愛

感

謝

Emoto masaru

5/07/0X

水からの伝言 vol.3

自分を愛するということ

The Message from Water vol.3

Love Thyself

✻ ✺ ❂

江本勝／IHM総合研究所

Masaru Emoto／IHM Research Institute

波動教育社

自分を愛するということ

水からの伝言 Vol.3

Love Thyself

The Message from Water Vol.3

戦争 / War

「戦争」という文字を水に見せました。
「平和」の結晶の中ほどが突き破られ、まるで 9.11. の世界貿易
センタービルにジェット旅客機が突っ込んだ瞬間のような結晶とな
りました。この写真は同年の 7 月に撮影されたものです。水は予知
能力があるかのようです。

We showed the word "War" to the water.
Smashing through the crystal of "Peace", a crystal formed resembling
the moment the jet airliners crashed into the World Trade Center
on September 11. This picture was taken in July of the same year. It
almost appears as if water has predictive abilities.

平和 / Peace

「平和」という文字を水に見せました。
「愛 感謝」の結晶が２つ重なり合ったような結晶ができました。

We showed the word "Peace" to the water.
A crystal that looked like a fusion of the crystals of "Love and Thanks"
appeared.

イマジン／ジョンレノン
Imagine／John Lennon

想像してごらん　天国なんてないんだと…
その気になれば簡単なことさ
僕らの足下には地獄はなく　頭上にはただ空があるだけ
想像してごらん　すべての人々が今日のために生きていると…

想像してごらん　国境なんてないんだと…
そんなに難しいことじゃない
殺したり死んだりする理由もなく　宗教さえもない
想像してごらん　すべての人々が平和な暮らしを送っていると…

想像してごらん　所有するものなんか何もないと…
果たしてきみにできるかな
欲張りや飢えの必要もなく　人はみな兄弟なのさ
想像してごらん　すべての人々が世界を分かち合っていると…

僕を夢想家だと思うかも知れない
だけど僕ひとりじゃないはずさ
いつの日か　きみも僕らに加われば
この世界はひとつに結ばれるんだ

Imagine there's no heaven　　　It's easy if you try
No hell below us　　Above us only sky
Imagine all the people　　Living for today …

Imagine there's no countries　　　It isn't hard to do
Nothing to kill or die for　　And no religion too
Imagine all the people　　Living life in peace …

Imagine no possessions　　　I wonder if you can
No need for greed or hunger　　A brotherhood of man
Imagine all the people　　Sharing all the world …

You may say I'm a dreamer　　　But I'm not the only one
I hope someday you'll join us　　　And the world will be as one

ジョン・レノンの「イマジン」を聴かせた水の結晶です。
この歌詞のように、束縛を受けず、各人が自由に成長する中で、
見事なハーモニーがかもしだされた、美しく個性的な結晶です。

This is the crystal exposed to the song,"Imagine" by John
Lennon. Like the words of this song, it is a beautiful and
unique crystal where each individual element grows freely
and with perfect harmony.

自分を愛するということ　　水からの伝言 Vol.3

戦争／平和／イマジン

はじめに

Love Thyself   The Message From Water Vol.3

War ╱ Peace ╱ Imagin

PREFACE

はじめに

　今年でわたしが開発した水の氷結結晶写真技術は10年になります。最初1台の大型冷蔵庫、1人の研究員ではじめたものが、今では3台の冷蔵庫と6人の研究員となり、その撮影の件数および枚数もかなり増えてまいりました。そして、何よりもその撮影技術において大変安定した結果を得られるようになり、研究の質もだいぶ向上してきたように思います。

　そして『水からの伝言』（波動教育社）を1999年6月に発表して以来、それはいつの間にか世界中に広がり、2004年1月現在で世界の17ヵ国語で翻訳出版されるようになりました。世界の人々の高い関心をかうことになったのです。それにつれて、わたしはいろいろな国から招かれて世界の国々を講演のため訪れるようになりました。その数は30ヵ国、150都市におよびます。

　どうしてこのようになったのでしょう。

　最初は夢中でしたからそれを考える余裕もなかったのですが、その後いろいろな国の人たちとお会いし、お話しているうちに、あるいはメールやお手紙をたくさんもらううちに、今ではその理由が良くわかり、わかればわかるほど自分の役割の大きさに気づかされたのです。そして、その責任に身震いし、使命感に燃えてきたのです。

　その理由とは、おもなだけでも箇条書きにまとめれば次のようなことです。

　すべて講演会の会場に直接来られた方たちからと、メールや手紙で寄せられた感想です。

① 世界の人びとが求めていた共通の言語が水の結晶の中にあった。
② 日ごろ考えていたことを水が代弁してくれた。
③ 自分の中に潜在的にあった記憶を水は覚醒してくれた。
④ 言葉の起源とその意味、大切さがわかった。
⑤ 音楽がなぜ人を癒すのかがわかった。
⑥ 絵画や彫刻、その他の芸術の持つ意味がわかった。
⑦ なぜ生命現象に水が欠かせないのかがわかった。
⑧ 代替医療がなぜ存在し効果があるのかがわかった。

⑨ 宗教と祈りについて理解するヒントをもらえた。
⑩ エネルギーの本質について理解するヒントとなった。
⑪ 人間と宇宙の関係を理解するのに役立った。
⑫ 次元ということを理解するヒントになった。
⑬ 人はいずこより来て、何のためにここにいるか、そして死んだらどうなるのか、という人類永遠のテーマに1歩近づくことができた。

　そのほか、教育機関、農業、医業、環境コンサルタント、食品業、化学工業、先端技術、サービス業、衣料業など、ほとんどあらゆる業種に従事する方から、それぞれのお仕事に応用できるヒントが多数あったとの感想をいただいています。

　このような背景において、わたしは今回『水からの伝言』の第3集の出版企画をするにあたり、今の世界が最も緊急に必要としていることをテーマに選ぼうと思いました。

　それはむろん、世界から戦争やテロをなくすことです。

　そして、選んだのが「祈り」というテーマです。

　さらにそれを掘り下げて考えてみた結果、「祈り」が最も効果的に発信されるのは、みなさん1人ひとりが世界の人びとが平和に生活している姿をイメージしながら、「自分の愛のエネルギーを高めること」であると気がつきました。数々の水に対しての問いかけの結果、水から教えられたのです。

　そのような理由で、本書のタイトルを『水からの伝言　自分を愛するということ』としました。まず自分が輝いてポジティブな元気な愛に満ちた振動を持ちましょう。それには自分を愛すること、自分に感謝すること、そして、自分を尊敬することだと思います。そうすればおのずとその振動は世界、そして宇宙に発信され、その共鳴の大シンフォニーは、かならずこの地球を誰もが神より与えられた、それぞれの命をいとおしむような波動で包み込んでくれることでしょう。

　水であるわたし、江本勝からのメッセージです。

PREFACE

It has been ten years this year since I developed the techniques of frozen water crystal photography. What started with one large refrigerator and one research member has now become three refrigerators and six research members, and the number of pictures and specimens has been increasing dramatically. More than anything, we are now able to obtain very stable results through our photographic techniques, and I believe the quality of our research has shown great improvement.

After the publication of *The Message from Water* (HADO Kyoikusha) in June 1999, its popularity spread all over the world, and it has been published in seventeen different languages as of January 2004, and thus has been able to attract keen interest from all the peoples of the world. Along with this, I began to be invited by many countries to give lectures. The number of places I have visited has now reached 150 cities and 30 countries.

How did this happen? At the beginning I was so overwhelmed that I wasn't able to consider the reasons, but later, having met and talked with people from various countries and from receiving many emails and letters, I now know well the reason. The more I understood, the more I realized the greatness of my role. I quivered with the responsibility and burned with my sense of mission.

The followings are some of the main reasons, though it is not an exhausting list. They are all from feedback that I received from the people who came to the lectures or by emails and letters.

① The common language that the people of the world have been seeking for is found in water crystals.

② Water speaks for us what is in our mind.

③ Water awakens the subconscious memory in each person.

④ I have learned the origin, the meaning, and importance of language.

⑤ I now know why music heals people.

⑥ I have learned the meaning that paintings, sculptures, and other art have.

⑦ I now know why water is indispensable to the phenomenon of life.

⑧ I understand now why alternative therapies exist and why they are effective.

⑨ It helped me to understand religion and prayer.

⑩ It gave me a clue to understanding the nature of energy.

⑪ It helped me understand the relationship between humanity and the cosmos.

⑫ It gave me a clue to help me understand what dimensionality is.

⑬ I could come one step closer to understanding the eternal theme of humanity that asks where we come from, why we are here and what happens when we die.

In addition to the above, we have been receiving comments from people that say there are many suggestions that can be applied to their each job. These people are representatives of almost all industries: training organizations, agriculture, medicine, environmental consultation, food industries, chemical industries, high-tech, service industries, clothing industries and so forth.

Thus for the release of this, the third volume in my series of *The Message from Water,* I decided to choose as a theme what the world most urgently needs at present. That is, of course, the need to eliminate war and terrorism throughout the world.

The theme I have chosen is "prayer". When I thought about it more deeply, I realized that "prayer" is most effectively sent when each person in the world "raises their energy of love" by imagining a scene where the peoples of the world are living in peace. I have been taught this by water through the process of asking water many questions.

For this reason, I have set the title of this book as *The Message from Water – Love Thyself.* First you must shine with positive, high-spirited vibrations, full of love. In order to do that, I think it is important to love yourself, to be able to thank yourself, and respect yourself. If that is the case, then each of those vibrations will be sent out into the world and the cosmos, and the great symphony of that harmonic vibration will verily wrap our planet in with the waves such as those that cherish our Heaven-granted lives.

This is my message from myself as water, Masaru Emoto.

第一章　祈りのかたち

Chapter 1　　The Shape of Prayer

手を合わせて祈ったとき、人は神秘的な感覚に満たされました。
When prayed with the palms together, people were filled with spiritual feelings.

第一章　祈りのかたち

　わたしたち日本人は「祈り」の行為をデザインで表しなさいという命題を受けたら、誰でも両手を合わせた合掌の形を描くと思います。海外の方も風土や宗教によって、その形は若干違うことはあるにしても、ほぼ同様の形をみなさん選ぶことでしょう。

　でもなぜ手を合わせることが、祈りに結びつくのでしょうか？

　それも世界的にほぼ共通の風習としてあるのは、なぜなのでしょうか？人間というものは、何か根拠のあることでなければ、それを習慣化しません。きっとなるほどと思わせる何か理由があるはずです。

　それをわたしなりに理解したのは、エネルギーとは振動で、振動とは共鳴によって継続されるという考えに至ったときのことです。すなわち個ではエネルギーは発生しないわけです。右手だけではエネルギーの対流はままならず、左手を合わせてはじめてスムースな対流が生まれるのです。

　そして、古代の人びとはきっと太陽の光のエネルギーを、両手を大きく広げて受け、それを祈りとして他に発信するとき、その想いのエネルギーが純粋に発信されるよう静かに目を瞑り、手を合わせて祈ったのではないか、とわたしは理解したのです。

　この章では、祈りに関するテーマの実験から、たまたま得られた、手を合わせた「祈りのかたち」を持った結晶写真をご紹介します。これがたまたまであるのか、なるべくしてなったのか、あなたはどう思われるでしょうか。

CHAPTER 1 The Shape of Prayer

When Japanese are given an assignment to design the deed of "prayer", I think every one of us would draw a shape of palms put together. People from other countries would probably choose similar shapes, though they might vary slightly depending on the climate and the religion.

But why is putting the hands together connected to prayer? And that why does it exist almost as a common practice all over the world? People do not make it a custom unless there are some grounds. There must be some good reasons that are truly convincing.

I realized this for myself when I reached the idea that energy means vibrations, and vibrations continue by resonance. In other words, energy is not generated independently.

The right hand alone cannot create an energy current. Only with the left hand added is a smooth circulation created. And I realized that ancient people, perhaps to receive the energy of the sunlight, opened their hands widely, and when they sent it to others as prayer, they quietly closed their eyes and prayed with both hands together in order for their emotional energy to be sent out purely.

In this section I will introduce crystal pictures that happen to contain the shape of the praying hands from our experiments under the theme of "prayer". Were these just coincidence, or did they appear as they did because they should have? What do you think?

和　Wa (Harmony)

札幌在住の書家の書いた「和」という字（右頁）とワープロで打った「和」という字（左頁）をそれぞれ同じ水に見せました。ともに「祈りのかたち」の結晶となりましたが、右の方がより鮮明です。やはり書かれた方の心が強くでているようです。日本も昔は和の国、あるいは大和の国と呼ばれていましたが、すべての和を願う国民意識を高揚しようという心が、常にあったのでしょう。それをいつまでも忘れてはいけないと思います。まさに「和を以って尊しとす」ですね。

We showed the word "Wa (和)" written both by a calligrapher (right) and a word processor (left) to separate containers of distilled water. Both formed the crystal of the "shape of prayer". However right was clearer. As expected, the soul of the calligrapher can have a strong influence. Japan was once called the Country of Wa, or Country of Yamato (大和 , meaning Great Harmony). I believe that there was once a spiritual awareness that attempted to raise the people's consciousness to pray for harmony in all things. I think it is important to never forget that, no matter how much time has passed. Indeed, "Harmony is the Greatest of Virtues".

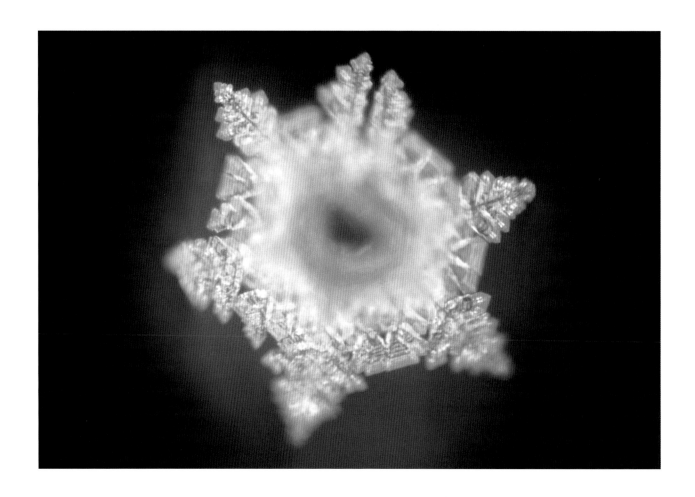

「グレゴリオ聖歌」 Gregorian Chant

西洋音楽の源泉といわれる「グレゴリオ聖歌」を水に聴かせた結晶です。カトリック教会の典礼音楽として千年以上、歌い継がれているようです。「アメイジング グレイス」と違い、天の方向一点に祈りが集中しています。この結晶は一生懸命歌っているように見えますね。

This is a crystal we found from the water to which we played Gregorian Chant. Considered one of the foundations of classical Western music, Gregorian Chant has been sung for over a millennium as liturgical music of the Catholic Church. This crystal looks as if it were singing with all its soul. Differing from "Amazing Grace", the prayer is concentrated in one point in the heavens.

「アメイジング グレイス」　Amazing Grace

「アメイジング グレイス」を聴かせた水の結晶です。この有名なゴスペルの歌詞は、もと奴隷船の船長によって書かれたといわれています。嵐の中、自分だけが奇跡的に死を免れたそうです。そして後に神に償い、感謝し、牧師になったといいますが、きっといろいろな意味で祈りが込められた詩なのでしょう。天と地に対して象徴的な「祈りのかたち」が現れています。

This is a crystal of water exposed to the sound of "Amazing Grace". It has been said that the words of this famous Gospel were written by a former master of a slave ship. It has also been said that he was, miraculously, the only survivor of a storm. Later he atoned his sins with God, and in thanks became a priest. The lyrics are bound to be full of many different meanings of prayer. Again, Heaven and the Earth appear in this typical "shape of prayer".

アーメン　Amen

キリスト教で唱える万国共通のこの言葉を、原語はヘブライ語ですが、日本語で「アーメン」と書いた文字を見せた結晶です。祈りや賛美歌を唱和した後にかならず、「今申し上げましたことは、間違いありません」という確認の意味で使われます。でも、わたしたちには祈りの言葉そのものに聞こえます。

We showed the word, "Amen" written in Japanese. Amen is Hebrew originally, but is now used universally with Christianity. It is used to confirm that "what we have just said is true" at the end of every prayer and choral hymn. To us, however, it sounds like the word of prayer it self.

魚のマーク   Fish Mark

キリスト教は初期の頃、「魚のマーク」で表わされたといいます。「魚」はギリシャ語で「イキトゥス」といわれ、「イエス、キリスト、神、息子、救い主」のギリシャ語のイニシャルを順に並べたものと同じであったことに起因するといわれていますが、最初のイエスの弟子4人がみな漁師であったのもおもしろい符合ですね。

Early Christians used the mark of a fish to represent Christ. This is said to be due to the fact that the Greek for "fish", "Ichthys", is an acrostic for "Iesous Christos Theou Yios Soter", or "Jesus Christ, Son of God, Saviour". And it is an interesting coincidence that the first four disciples of Jesus Christ were all fishermen.

合掌　Gassho (hands joined in prayer)

「合掌」という文字を見せたら、「祈りのかたち」は四方に伸びてゆきました（左頁）。その後、その思いが通じたのでしょうか、ごらんのような豪華絢爛たる結晶に成長していったのです（写真上）。よく見ると水の神といわれる「竜神」のような顔をしています。

Exposed to the word "Gassho", the "shape of prayer" in the crystal stretched out in all directions (left). Maybe the feeling of true hope was reached because later it grew to become an absolutely gorgeous crystal, as you can see in the right picture. Looking at it carefully, it almost looks like the face of "Ryujin (the Dragon God of Water)".

自己愛　Jikoai (Self-love)

「自己愛」という文字を水に見せました。自分を愛せなくては、他人を愛することはできません。自分が輝いてこそ、別の言葉でいうならば、自分の振動が元気いっぱいでなければ、他のものに振動を与えることはできないのです。まず、「己(おのれ)の中で共鳴し振動しましょう」「己の中で手を合わせましょう」と水はいっているようです。

We showed the word "Self-love" to the water. If we are unable to love ourselves, we cannot truly have the ability to love others. We must be shining, or in other words, our vibrations should be full of energy; otherwise we cannot resonate with others. The water seems to be saying, "first resonate and vibrate in yourself - clasp your hands within yourself".

共鳴　　Kyomei（Resonance）

「共鳴」という文字を水に見せました。やはり共鳴の源泉は天にあるのでしょう。それを
受けてすべてのものが手をつなぎ、和しているようです。中央は日輪のようにみえます。

We showed the word "Resonance" to the water. Perhaps the source of resonance can be found within Heaven. All things seem to be receiving that resonance, holding hands and harmonizing. I believe "Nichirin (the sun)" is in the center of the crystal.

幣立神宮 <ruby>へ<rt></rt></ruby>　Heitate Shrine

幣立神宮の写真を見せた水の結晶です。わたしは縁あって10年ほど前から、この神宮を訪れるようになり、なんと137代目宮司と、その宿坊である世界平和道場の道場主と懇意になり、日本古神道についてさまざまなことを学びました。それらが、わたしのバックボーンの1つとなっているように思います。この結晶が、わたしがはじめて「祈りのかたち」を意識した写真です。

This is a crystal from water exposed to the picture of the Heitate Shrine. For various reasons, I have been visiting this shrine regularly for the past decade, and was fortunate to get acquainted with the 137th chief priest as well as the director of the shrine guesthouse, Sekai Heiwa Dojo (the World Peace Training Hall). Here I learned many things about Ancient Shin-to. I think these things have partly become the backbone of my philosophical approach. This is the first crystal picture that made me fully aware of the "shape of prayer".

幣立神宮	九州の熊本県蘇陽町にあり、高天原神話発祥のお宮で、天照大神を主祭神として祀っている。
Heitate Shrine	Situated in the town of Soyo, Kumamoto Prefecture, in Kyushu, and is where the Takamagahara myth is said to have originated. It is dedicated to Amaterasu Omikami (the Sun Goddess).

ヤハウエ　Jehovah

ヤハウエはユダヤ教の神で万物の創造主、宇宙の統治者とされています。この写真はヘブライ語の「ヤハウエ」という文字を見せた水の結晶です。「幣立神宮」の写真を見せた結晶と、とても似ています。一部の超古代史研究者は、古代大和（日本）と古代ユダヤ民族について、兄弟的な関係であったとしていますが、はたして……。

Jehovah is the God of Judaism and is regarded as the creator of all nature and the supreme ruler of the universe. This is a picture of a water crystal exposed to the Hebrew letters "Jehovah". As previously stated, this has a close resemblance with the crystal of the Heitate Shrine picture. Some scholars of ancient history suggest the ancient Yamato people (Japanese) and the ancient Jewish people were closely related, like brothers; however, this is most certainly a very debatable point….

南北統一　Nanboku Toitsu（Unification of North and South）

この文字はハングル語で水に見せました。ですから南北朝鮮の統一を願う心が表れていると
いえますが、特に、韓国側の人びとの思いが代弁されていると思います。『水からの伝言』
の韓国語版出版の際に、韓国の出版社の人に「南北統一」というテーマを選んでもらったか
らです。祈りの方向が真北に向いているのはそのためでしょうか。

We showed this phrase written in Korean to the water. For that reason, I truly believe that this
expresses the deep desire for the unification of North and South Korea. This perhaps more fully
represents the thoughts and sentiment of the South Korean people, because we asked our Korean
publishing company to choose "Unification of North and South" for the theme of the Korean
version of *The Message from Water*. Is that the reason why the prayer is directed due north?

阪神優勝

The Hanshin Tigers - Baseball Champions

日本のプロ野球チーム阪神は、関西地区の熱狂的なファンの応援のおかげで、2003 年に 18 年ぶりのリーグ優勝を果たしました。「阪神優勝」という文字を見せた水の結晶は、「祈りのかたち」の上に 3 段重ねとなりました。わたしには 1 番下が熱心な阪神ファンの祈りで、それによってチームが支えられ、監督さんが胴上げされたように見えます。

The Hanshin Tigers, a Japanese professional baseball team, captured the 2003 league tournament championship for the first time in 18 years. Enthusiastic fans in the Kansai area supported them. The crystal of water exposed to the characters formed a three-tiered structure. To me, it looks like that the bottom tier is the prayer of the enthusiastic Hanshin fans, the next layer is the team being supported by them, then on the top is the coach being tossed in the air in celebration.

第二章　祈りのたまてばこ

Chapter 2　　　A Cornucopia of Prayer

宗教的な言葉も祈りも音楽も、みなそれぞれに素晴らしい。
Religious words, prayers and music are all wonderful.

第二章　祈りのたまてばこ

　この章では、日本をはじめ世界各国の祈りに関係する、言葉や、音楽や、写真を水に見せたり、聴かせたりした結晶を取り上げてお見せします。

　それらに対するさまざまな水の反応から、何を感じられるでしょうか。わたしが感じたことをご紹介させていただきますが、それらは感じかたの１つであって、あなたが感じられたこと、それが、水があなたに伝えたいことです。

CHAPTER 2
A Cornucopia of Prayer

This chapter provides you with a random selection of the crystals we found when we showed and played words and phrases, music, and pictures of Japan and other countries in the world that are related to prayer. I would like to ask that you try and feel something from the various reactions of water to them. Here, I present you with what I felt, but it is only an example of what we might feel. What you yourself feel is what the water means to tell you.

般若心経　Han-nya-shin-gyo

<ruby>般若心経<rt>はんにゃしんぎょう</rt></ruby>

般若心経266文字を見せた水の結晶です。セブンチャクラの7番目の
チャクラである<ruby>頭頂葉<rt>とうちょうよう</rt></ruby>が活性化したというイメージを、わたしは持ちま
した。そこは宇宙全体との一体感を連携するポイントといわれています。

This is a water crystal produced from the 266 characters of the Heart Sutra.
I have a feeling that the seventh chakra of seven chakras, the parietal lobe,
has been activated. It is supposed to be your link to oneness with the entire
cosmos.

般若心経	古代インドで成立した仏教経典。深遠な<ruby>智慧<rt>ちえ</rt></ruby>を凝縮させた<ruby>経文<rt>きょうもん</rt></ruby>は、日本人に最も広く親しまれ、日本仏教のほとんどの宗派において<ruby>読誦<rt>どくしょう</rt></ruby>、<ruby>写経<rt>しゃきょう</rt></ruby>されている。
Han-nya-shin-gyo	Buddhist scriptures from ancient India. This sutra, full of esoteric wisdom, is the most widely known among Japanese, and they are recited and transcribed in almost all denominations of Japanese Buddhism.

セブンチャクラ	人には精神と身体に関連した生命エネルギーが7つあると考えられ、背骨の基底部から数えて、第1チャクラから頭頂部の第7チャクラまであるとされる。
Seven chakras	A man has seven vital energy centers related to the mind and body, starting from the 1st charka at the bottom of the spine to the 7th charka at the parietal lobe.

文字を見せる

色即是空 空即是色 — Shiki-soku-ze-ku Ku-soku-ze-shiki

<ruby>色<rt>しき</rt>即<rt>そく</rt>是<rt>ぜ</rt>空<rt>くう</rt></ruby> <ruby>空<rt>くう</rt>即<rt>そく</rt>是<rt>ぜ</rt>色<rt>しき</rt></ruby>

この言葉は、わたしの解釈では、量子力学用語だと思っています。すべては超高速で振動点滅しているという、量子の世界の物理現象を表した素晴らしい表現です。結晶の中央に見える黒い空洞が「空」で、美しい枝葉が「色」だと思います。

I interpret this phrase as being associated with quantum mechanics. It is a wonderful expression of the physical phenomenon of the quantum world, where everything switches on and off at extreme speed. I think that the dark hollow you can see in the middle of the crystal is "Ku", emptiness, and the beautiful branches are "Shiki", form.

色即是空　空即是色　般若心経にある句。「色即是空」は、すべての存在は一切これという実体がない。「空即是色」は、すべては実体がないけれども、それぞれの存在には意味があり光り輝いているの意。

Shiki-soku-ze-ku Ku-soku-ze-shiki　A phrase within Han-nya-shin-gyo, "Shiki-soku-ze-ku" means existence is without form. "Ku-soku-ze-shiki" means formless is existence, and each existence has meaning; is shining.

南無妙法蓮華経
（なむみょうほうれんげきょう）

Namu-myoho-renge-kyo

「南無妙法蓮華経」という文字を水に見せました。日蓮聖人（にちれんしょうにん）はこのお経を、ただひたすら無心に唱えなさいと教えました。たしかにその意味がわからなくとも、いつも身近に感じていたいような素晴らしく、また美しい結晶です。

We showed the phrase "Namu-myoho-renge-kyo" to the water. Nichiren's teachings were to repeatedly chant this sutra unselfconsciously. Indeed without knowing the exact meaning, this is a perfect and gorgeous crystal and the kind of crystal that makes us want to keep it close to us all the time.

南無妙法蓮華経　　鎌倉時代に仏教信仰者日蓮によってはじめて唱えられた。法華経（ほけきょう）を信仰し加護（かご）を求める心持ちを表して唱える語。御題目（おだいもく）。

Namu-myoho-renge-kyo　Chanted for the first time by Nichiren, a Buddhist believer in the Kamakura period, about eight hundred years ago. It is a phrase that expresses the believer's desire to call upon the Lotus Sutra for help and protection.

文字を見せる

Showing Words

南無阿弥陀仏
Namu-amida-butsu

「南無阿弥陀仏」という文字を水に見せました。それぞれの6角の根元から内側のコアに向かって伸びている光は魂の音叉のようです。それを受けて中央にはピンクと緑の色。波動的にはピンクは愛、緑は感謝の色です。

The light stretching toward the inner core from each of the six bottom corners is like a tuning fork. The recipient, in the center, is colored pink and green. In my HADO theory, pink is love and green is thanks.

南無阿弥陀仏 　　平安末期、法然によって開かれた仏教の一派である浄土宗で唱えられた。阿弥陀仏に帰依するの意。念仏。

Namu-amida-butsu 　Chanted by the Pure Land sect of Buddhism (Jodo-shu), a sect of Buddhism established by Honen at the end of the Heian period, over eight hundred years ago. It means to become a devotee of the Buddha Amida. It is often known as the "nenbutsu", or "invocation".

文字を見せる

Showing Words

あまてらすおおみかみ
天照大神

「天照大神」という文字を水に見せました。天照大神は文字通り日の神で、昔は日本の主神とされていましたが、この結晶を見たときの驚きは、たいへんなものがありました。まず、わたしくらいの年齢のものには、こんな実験をやっては罰が当たるのではないか、という思いがあるのですが、この結果を得て、結晶写真そのものに対して、信頼と畏敬の念を持つようになりました。右ページの結晶は、温度の上昇により成長したものですが、まさに三種の神器のうちの1つ「鏡」そのものです。

天照大神　　記紀神話に登場する太陽神的な神の名。古事記によればイザナギノミコトが禊で左目を洗った際に成り出たという。

文字を見せる
Showing Words

Amaterasu Omikami

We showed the words "Amaterasu Omikami" to the water. Amaterasu Omikami literally means the Goddess of the Sun, and was once regarded as the central deity in the Japanese pantheon. I was most surprised when I saw this crystal. First of all, many people at my age are worried that doing an experiment like this is akin to blasphemy, but with the results of this experiment, I came to have a sense of confidence and awe towards the crystal photograph itself. Crystal below expanded as the temperature rose. It really is just like the Sacred Mirror, one of Three Sacred Treasures of Shin-to.

Amaterasu Omikami   Name of the sun goddess which appears in the Chronicles of Classical Japan. According to the Kojiki, the "Record of Ancient Matters", it appeared when Izanagino Mikoto washed his left eye in the purification ceremony.

すさのおのみこと　Susanoono Mikoto

天照大神の弟といわれる「すさのおのみこと」は剣^{つるぎ}がその象徴とされていますが、この写真からも、たしかに剣のイメージは感じられます。しかし、それは剛というより、柔という感じです。

The sword is the symbol of "Susanoono Mikoto", said to be the brother of Amaterasu Omikami (the Sun Goddess). This picture does give the impression of a sword, but it seems soft rather than brutal.

文字を見せる

アソヒノオオカミ　Asohino Okami

前述した幣立神宮の137代目春木宮司は、この写真をはじめて見たときに「これはアソヒノオオカミではないですか」といわれました。事前に何もお知らせしていなかったものですからびっくりし、結晶写真の感性の正確さに、自信をもったという経緯があります。

Shinya Haruki, the chief priest of the Heitate Shrine mentioned earlier, seeing this picture for the first time, said, "Isn't this Asohino Okami?" I had not told him beforehand, so I was very surprised, and gained confidence in the precise sensitivity of the crystal pictures.

アソヒノオオカミ	幣立神宮に伝わる石版に書かれている古代文字。宇宙神が日の玉に移って地に降り、お宮を造り神の元としたという。
Asohino Okami	Ancient letters written on a slate palette housed at the Heitate Shrine. The God of the Universe came down to Earth riding on the ball of the sun and created a shrine to make the base of the gods.

ハッピークリスマス（英語）

Happy Christmas（English）

英語の「ハッピークリスマス」という文字を水に見せました。英国紳士のように端正な美しさを見せています。均整の取れた美しさの中に、ハッピーを求めるといった感じです。

English Happy Christmas possesses a noble beauty like that of an English gentleman. It has a feeling of seeking happiness within beauty.

文字を見せる

ハッピークリスマス（イタリア語）

Happy Christmas (Italian)

同じ意味でも、言語によってこうも変わるのですね。奔放（ほんぽう）に、そして少し破目を外してクリスマスを楽しんでいるかのようです。誰ですか？　イタリア人らしいといっているのは。

It varies depending on the language, dose it not? This looks like the idea of enjoying Christmas by indulging in merry-making. What, you think that sounds very Italian?

胎蔵界曼荼羅　Taizoukai Mandala

真言密教に伝えられる曼荼羅のうちの1つですが、それが何を意味するのか、まだ、わたしにはわかりません。ただ、「胎蔵界曼荼羅」の写真を見せた結晶は「お母さん」（写真左下）という文字を見せた結晶に良く似ており、やさしく包み込む慈愛に満ちたものとなっています。中央の空洞の向こうから生まれいずる、生命誕生の図のようでもあります。

The Taizoukai is one of the mandalas for Shingon esoteric Buddhism. I still do not know what it means. However, the crystal from the water exposed to the picture of Taizoukai Mandala looks very similar to the crystal I grew after showing the word for "Mother(left below)", full of mercy that wraps you around gently. It also looks like the picture of birth of a new life coming from the central hollow.

胎蔵界曼荼羅　　仏教の経典「大日経」の説に基づく。胎蔵界を図示したもの。
Taizoukai Mandala　　Based on the comment in the "Dainichikyo", a Buddhist sutra. Illustration of Taizoukai.

シンボルを見せる

金剛界曼荼羅 Kongoukai Mandala

叡智を表す曼荼羅と解説されていますが、「三人寄れば文殊の知恵」といった感じでしょうか。感覚的には、胎蔵界と金剛界を一緒にしたら完成するように思えます。

This Mandala is explained as a mandala of wisdom and insight. It is perhaps rather like "out of the counsel of three comes wisdom". I feel instinctively that it will form a complete whole if the Taizoukai and Kongoukai are combined.

金剛界曼荼羅　仏教の経典「金剛頂経」の説に基づく。金剛界を図示したもの。その内容を九つの部分に分けることから九会曼荼羅ともいう。

Kongoukai Mandala　Based on the comment in "Kongochokyo", a Buddhist sutra. Illustration of Kongokai. As it is divided into nine parts, it is also called the Kue Mandala (ku meaning nine).

陰陽　InYo

陰陽の解釈はとても難解です。ただ、大陽の中の小陰、大陰の中の小陽というところにキーポイントがあるように思えます。「陰陽」の文字を見せた水の結晶はそれに近いものになりました。

The interpretation of InYo (Ying and Yang) principles is very difficult, but I think the key point with it lies with the small In in large Yo and the small Yo in large In. The water crystal exposed to the characters of InYo turned out very close to that meaning.

陰陽　　東洋哲学における宇宙の根本原理。すべての事物や現象は「陰」と「陽」との二気から生じ、また「陰」と「陽」との相対的な関係を以って存在しているとする。

InYo　　The fundamental principal of the universe in Oriental philosophy. All materials and phenomena occur from two types of qi, "In (Ying)" and "Yo (Yang)", and exist in the relative relations of "In" and "Yo".

シンボルを見せる

ハートのマーク　Heart Mark

「ハート」のマークを水に見せたら、水はこんな結晶をつくりました。まず、これは日本語の「心」という字に似ています。そして、その全体像はちょっといびつなハートのようでもありますね。左右2つにわかれた心臓のようにも見えます。水の結晶っておもしろいですね。

We showed the water a "Heart" mark and the water formed a crystal like this. First of all, this looks like the Japanese character 心 (Kokoro), which means "heart". And the shape overall is like a crooked heart. It also looks like an actual heart splitting into two. Water crystals can be a great deal of fun, I feel.

十字架　Cross

ただ単に十字のマークを水に見せただけなのに、こんなに味わいのある結晶が撮れました。
１つの枝にだけ２つのコブがついています。きっと何か深い意味があるのでしょう。

We only showed a simple cross mark to the water, but it formed such a profound crystal as this.
We see two knots on only one of the branches. This must be implying something deep, I feel.

シンボルを見せる

バスマラ   Basmalah

バスマラはイスラム教徒にとって、とてもだいじな経文です。何か事を起こすとき、たとえば食事をとる前や、寝る前など、節目ごとにこれを唱えるといいます。「バスマラ」を見せた水は、ごらんのように申し分のない美しい結晶をつくりました。その意味は知りません。でも、こんなに良い結晶なら覚えたくなるような気がします。

Basmalah is a very important sutra passage for Muslims. It is recited before doing something, for example, before taking a meal, before going to bed and so forth. The water exposed to "Basmalah" crystallized as an impeccably beautiful crystal. I do not know the meaning of Basmalah, but now I feel I want to learn because of this beauty of this crystal.

ババジの絵「変化」

Pictures of Babaji "Change"

ババジという人（？）について、実はわたしはまったく知りませんでしたが、ヨーロッパのセミナー会場で、よく質問にでるので調べたところ、西暦200年代にインドで生まれた聖者で、不死身、現在1800歳くらいで、今なお健在といわれていることがわかりました。彼のことを信ずる方が、彼が書いたという画集をくださったので、わたしはそれを日本に持ち帰り、スタッフに写真を撮ってもらったところ、ごらんのように美しい6角形の結晶写真が連続して撮れたのです。あなたはどう思われますか？

シンボル（絵）を見せる

ババジの絵「真実」

Pictures of Babaji "Truth"

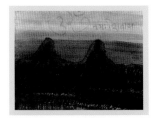

While in fact I had not originally known anything about a person (?) called Babaji, but since I received many questions regarding Babaji in the seminars in Europe, I investigated. I learned that Babaji is a holy man said to have been born in the 200s in India, and is said to be immortal. He is supposed to be still alive and about 1800 years old. A person who believes in him brought a book of paintings they said Babaji drew. I brought it back to Japan and had a picture taken by a member of my staff. The result was that we achieved a series of beautiful hexagonal crystals such as these. What do you think?

ダビデ David

このマークは良いエネルギーをつくりだす幾何学模様<ruby>幾何学模様<rt>きかがくもよう</rt></ruby>のようです。なぜなら、この写真を撮ったのは、今年の春入社予定の研修生さんだからです。３角形は「ひふみ」に通じるのでしょう。それが２つ入り組んで、はじめて共鳴現象を起こし、３時限的なエネルギーを創造する。そのように考えています。

There is no doubt that this mark is a geometric pattern that creates good energy, because this picture was taken by a trainee who is going to enter our company this spring. Two triangles have to be incorporated to resonate to create three-dimensional energy. That is at least what I think.

シンボルを見せる

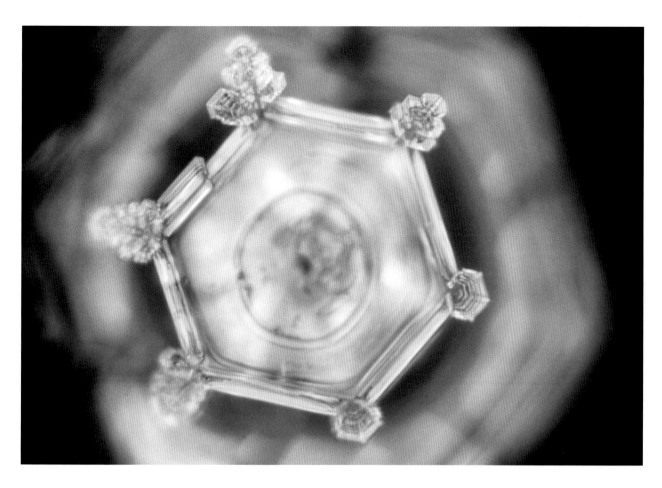

救霊符　Kyureifu

<ruby>救<rt>きゅう</rt></ruby><ruby>霊<rt>れい</rt></ruby><ruby>符<rt>ふ</rt></ruby>

知人がわたしのために持ってきてくれたものです。たしかに魂が守られているような構図の結晶となりました。背景の大きな結晶は背後霊かも !?

An acquaintance of mine brought this talisman to me. And indeed, the crystal turned out to be structured like a soul being protected. Might the large crystal in the back be a background spirit?

救霊符　　道教で発達した、神仙に願いを聞き届けてもらうための符だ。自然界の霊気や神仙の力を写し取ったものとされる。

Kyureifu　A talisman developed in Taoism in order to have prayers granted by the Immortals. It is regarded as the reflection of the aura of the natural world and power of the Immortals.

仏教　Buddhism

仏教の文字を見せた水の結晶は、コアが空洞となりました。あの世を認める仏教、この空洞はその連絡の道なのでしょうか。

The crystals that were achieved by showing water the word "Buddhism" had a hollow core in the middle. Buddhism recognizes the Other World. Is this hollow a connection to the other world?

キリスト教　Christianity

華やかなクリスマスツリーがいっぺんに6本もできてしまったようですが、その1つひとつの飾りはまことに精妙で美しいものがありますね。キリストの心とはきっとこのように高貴な美しさだったのでしょう。

It seems like six gorgeous Christmas trees have formed simultaneously, and each individual tree is truly exquisitely beautiful.

ユダヤ教　Judaism

2重の美しい構造ですが、背後にあるのはやはり大きな「祈りのかたち」をした結晶です。そのエネルギーは、ほとばしるように旺盛です。

It has a beautiful overlapping structure. The rear crystal is a large one, which also has the "shape of prayer". It is fountaining out energy.

イスラム教　Islam

中央の支柱ともいうべき部分は虹色に輝いています。また1つひとつの枝の先端は、他の宗教の場合と同じように力強く上に上にと伸張してゆくさまをみせています。

The central pillar is shining in rainbow colors and each branch tip extends powerfully upward, just like the crystals of the other religions.

ヒンドゥー教　Hinduism

全体が柔らか味のある円い形が特徴です。いろいろな宗派からなるインドの宗教ということですが、たしかに統合という感じを受けます。

It has a nice, gentle round look overall. There are various Hindu denominations in India, but this crystal gives an impression of unification.

宗教名を見せる

a　仏教　Buddhism

b　キリスト教　Christianity

c　ユダヤ教　Judaism

d　イスラム教　Islam

e　ヒンドゥー教　Hinduism

a　b　c　d　e

仏教	Buddhism
キリスト教	Christianity
ユダヤ教	Judaism
イスラム教	Islam
ヒンドゥー教	Hinduism

５つの宗教の文字をすべて一緒に水に見せてみました。６角形の１つの角は幻のようにぼやけていて、まるで５感に対する第６感のようです。

We showed the names of all five religions all at once to the water. Normally it should be hexagonal, but one of the corners is hazy like an illusion, as if it were the sixth sense to our normal five senses.

宗教名を見せる
Showing the Names of Religions

666 と 369 の数字を水に見せたら…

When we showed the numbers 666 and 369 …

666

ヨハネの黙示録に出てくる悪魔の数字といわれる「666」を水に見せました。全体的に汚れた結晶しかできなかったのですが、あえてこの写真を選びました。悪魔的というのはこのように、見方によっては魅力的なものがあると思えるからです。

We showed the number 666, which appears as the Number of the Devil in Revelations. In general, it created only dirty crystals, but I dared to select this picture because I think that depending on the way you look at it there can be something attractive with being demonic, as you see with this photo.

369

それに対応するといわれる数字「369」を水に見せました。666引くことの369を一桁ずつ引き算をします。6－3＝3　6－6＝0　6－9＝－3で合計で0となり悪い現象が相殺されるというのです。日本の弥勒菩薩はこの数字を語源としているという説を唱える人もいます。たしかにごらんのようにとても美しく、また中央には大黒さまのような顔がみえます。

We showed the number 369, which is regarded as being the opposite to 666. Subtracting 369 from 666 in each column makes 6-3=3, 6-6=0, 6-9=-3, which makes 0 in total, leading to the annihilation of evil phenomena. There is a view that the Japanese Buddha of the Future, the Miroku Bosatsu(mi-ro-ku sounds similar to three-six-nine in Japanese) is derived from this number. Indeed, as you see, the crystal is very beautiful, and in the center you can see a face like the Daikoku God of Fortune.

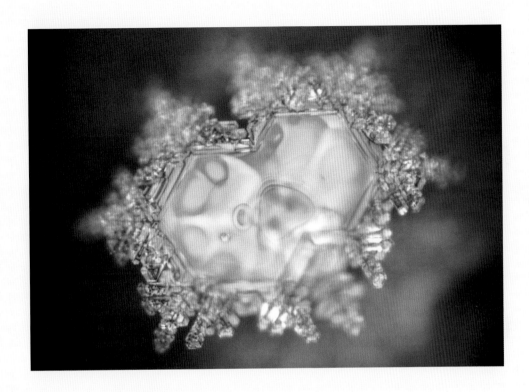

666
369

「666」と「369」を同時に水に見せました。そうしましたら、ごらんのようにツイン形の美しい結晶ができました。どうやら弥勒菩薩伝説は正しいのかもしれません。666という数字にアレルギーを持つ方には朗報です。

We showed the water 666 and 369 at the same time. The result was, as you see, a beautiful twin-shaped crystal. It may be possible that the Miroku Bosatsu legend is correct. This is good news for the people who have been phobic to the number 666.

ヨハネ黙示録　　1世紀末のキリスト教黙示文学。新約聖書中の一書で、その最後に置かれる。

Revelations　　Christian Revelation literature from the end of the first century. This is a letter by John placed last in the New Testament, though a different John from the Gospel according to John.

「声明」 Shomyo

「しょうみょう」と読みます。わかりやすくいえば、法要で僧侶たちが唱えるお経の合唱です。「散華」といって蓮の花びらを散らしながら歌う声明を水に聴かせてみました。やはり連なるという感じですね。この声明に導かれて、あの世に行くことができるのでしょうか。

Simply put, it is a chorus of sutra chanted by priests for memorial services. We played for the water a Shomyo called "Scattering Flowers" that is sung while scattering lotus petals. As expected, they lie in series. Would it be possible to ascend to Heaven if led by this Shomyo?

音楽を聴かせる

「君が代」 Japanease National Anthem, Kimigayo

君が代（歌詞付き）を聴いた蒸留水はとても美しい結晶をつくりました。しかし、この曲を聴くことによって悲しくつらいことを思い出してしまう人がいるのも事実です。当然そのような人の身体の中の水は違う結晶となるのかもしれません。

The distilled water that had been exposed to the sound of Kimigayo (with the lyrics) formed a beautiful crystal. It is, however, also a fact that some people are reminded of an unpleasant past by listening to this song. The water in such people's bodies may naturally form different crystals.

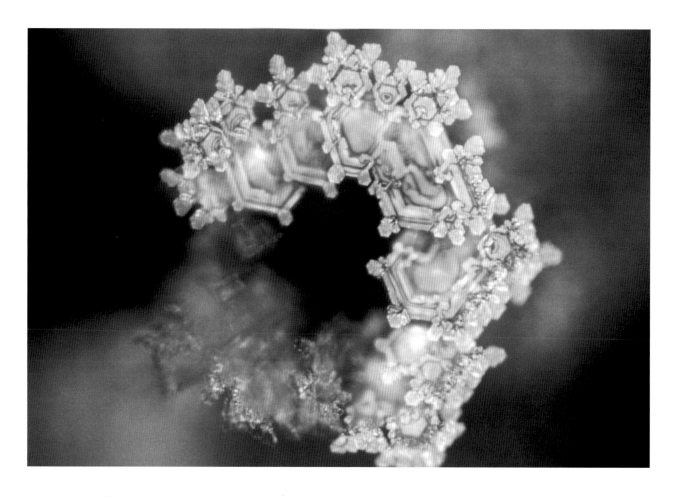

「アヴェ マリア」 ／グノー作曲　スーザン・オズボーン歌

Ave Maria　　　　Composed by Gounod / Sung by Suzan Osbourne

映画　地球交響曲「ガイアシンフォニー」のテーマ曲にもなった、スーザン・オズボーンさんが歌ったグノーの「アヴェ マリア」を水に聴かせた結晶です。彼女がわたしどものオフィスに来られたときに、この写真をお見せしたところ、彼女は感極まって泣き出してしまいました。彼女がこの歌を歌うときの情感が、そのまま表れているということでした。それにしても、たしかに魂を揺さぶられるような結晶です。

This is a crystal produced by playing Gounod's "Ave Maria", the theme music of the movie "Gaia Symphony" as sung by Suzan Osbourne. When she came to our office and we showed her this picture, she was so moved that she burst into tears. She said that the crystal expresses precisely the feelings she has when she sings this song. At any rate, this crystal seems to stir our souls.

音楽を聴かせる

「きよしこの夜」 Silent Night

中央にはほんとうに美しい真珠が現れました。たしかにこの曲を聴くと真珠のように心が洗われる感じがします。

In the center appeared a truly beautiful pearl. When we listen to this song , indeed we feel our souls to be washed off.

「コーラン」 The Koran

イスラム経の聖典「コーラン」のテープを水に聴かせてみました。楽器はいっさい用いず、朗々と<ruby>朗々<rt>ろうろう</rt></ruby>と歌い上げるところが特徴的でしたが、たいへん象徴的なデザインの結晶となりました。

We played to the water a tape of the Koran. It was characteristic in being sung sonorously without any musical accompaniment. The crystal turned out to have a very symbolic design.

音楽を聴かせる

Playing Music to Water

東京　国分寺・真姿の池

Masugata Pond at the Kokubunji, Tokyo

国分寺といえば巨大都市東京のベッドタウンです。通常ですと、その真ん中にある池の水がこれほど美しい結晶をみせるとは考えられません。生活雑廃水などがどうしても入り込んでしまうからです。実は、この水はわたしが採水してきたのですが、この水のある公園はなんとも波動の良いところで、多くの市民が水辺で憩うていました。上手に水と語り合えるような形に設計されていました。

Kokubunji is a commuter town in the Tokyo megalopolis. Normally we would not expect to see pond water in the middle of this town makes a crystal as beautiful as this, because the water would inevitably be contaminated by various kinds of domestic sewage. Actually, I drew this water from the pond. The park where the water is has good HADO and many people were relaxing there. It was landscaped very well to allow good communication with the water.

場を感じる

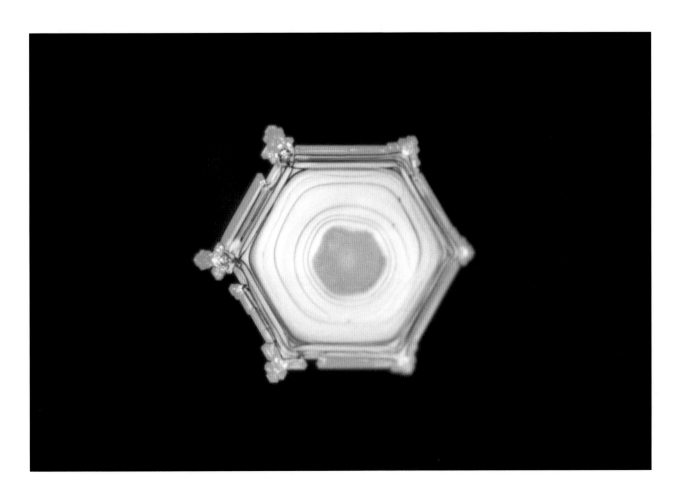

熊野　玉置神社の湧き水

Spring Water of Tamaki Shrine, Kumano

熊野の奥の宮といわれている玉置神社の湧き水の結晶写真です。コアが５重の層をもつ特異な形をみせてくれましたが、これはいったい、なにを訴えているのでしょうか？　さらなるデータの集積により、いろいろ神秘的なことがわかってくると思いますが、楽しい仕事であり研究です。

This is a crystal picture of the spring water in Tamaki Shrine known as the Inner Sanctum of Kumano. This gave us a unique shape with a core in five layers. What is this telling us ? With further data collection, I believe that the various mysteries will be revealed. This is both a fun occupation as well as research.

玉置神社　　和歌山県十津川村、玉置山の山頂直下に鎮座している。主祭神は国常立尊。

Tamaki Shrine　　Situated immediately beneath the top of Tamaki Mountain in Totsugawa village, Wakayama, and dedicated to the god Kunitokotachino Mikoto.

韓国　羅州の奇跡の泉 Miracle Spring in Naju, Korea

ある日、1人の青年が韓国からこの水を持参してきました。なんでも韓国の「ルルドの泉」といわれる水だそうです。本人は立派な会社のエリートエンジニアだったのですが、同時に熱心なクリスチャンでもありました。この結果をみて、彼はその会社を辞めてしまい、新しい仕事に就きました。1枚の美しい水の結晶が人の運命を変えることは少なくありません。かく申すわたしがそうでした。

One day a young man brought this water from Korea. We were told that the water is known as the Korean "Spring of Lourdes". This young man was an elite engineer from a good company and at the same time he was a devout Christian. Seeing this result, he left his company and changed jobs. It is not unusual for a single beautiful water crystal to change a person's destiny. It certainly happened in my case.

羅州奇跡の水　　　韓国の羅州に住んでいる女性が、聖母マリアから啓示を受けて、指示された場所を掘ったところ水が湧きだした。
現在でも毎日ソウルからバスでたくさんの人が訪れており、さまざまな奇跡が起こっているという。

Naju Miracle Water　A woman who lived in Naju, Korea, received a revelation from the Virgin Mary and dug as instructed, and water gushed out.
Even now many people visit from Seoul by bus daily and claim various miracles happen.

場を感じる

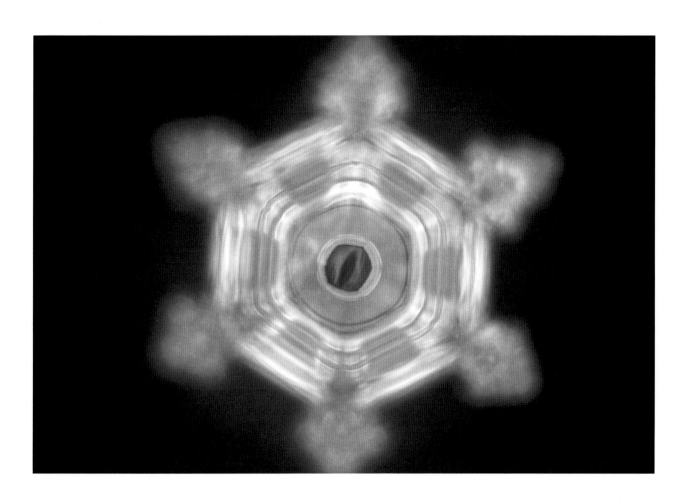

アメリカ　ナイアガラの滝

Niagara Falls, America

滝に打たれての荒行（あらぎょう）は何よりも良い精神修練効果を生む、あるいは滝壺の近くはマイナスイオンがいっぱいで、よい気に満ちているといわれていますが、まさにそれを裏づけるような結晶となりました。中央のコアは龍神の目のようです。

The cold water ascetic practice of sitting under a waterfall provides the most effective mental training. It is said that the basin is full of negative ions and good qi. The crystal we received substantiated this. The core in the center looks like the eye of a dragon.

サウジアラビア
ザムザムの泉

在日のアラブの方とご縁ができて、お持ちい
ただいた、サウジアラビアのジェッダ近郊に
湧く聖水の結晶です。原水は含有成分が多い
ため1000倍に希釈したものです。砂漠の中
の水とは思えないその美しい結晶は、なぜか、
常に重なり合ったものとなりました。

Zamzam, Saudi Arabia

This is a crystal of the sacred spring water near
Jetta in Saudi Arabia brought by an Arab person
living in Japan, with whom I had a chance to get
acquainted. The raw water has many particles,
so we used water diluted a thousand times.
This beautiful water from the desert turned out
overlapping forms every time, which made us
wonder why.

場を感じる

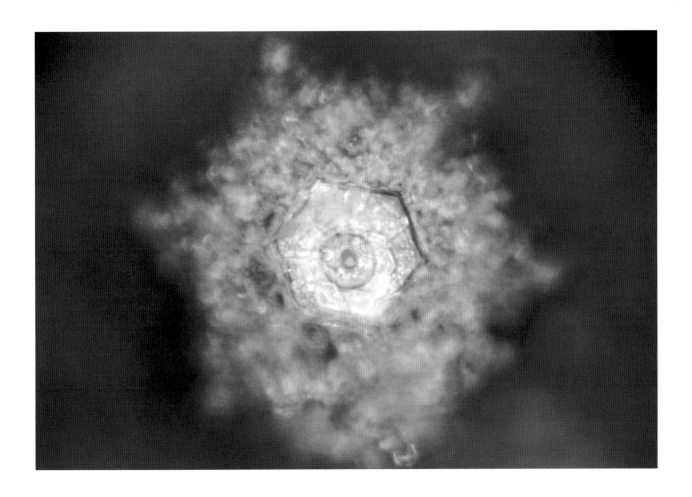

サウジアラビア　メッカ

Mecca, Saudi Arabia

イスラム教の聖地「メッカ」の写真を見せました。他にもメッカの写真が何点かあったのですが、そのうちの1つ、上空から撮ったものに、そっくりの結晶となりましたので、たいへん驚きました。もちろん、水に見せている写真の雰囲気も怖いほどでています。

We showed a picture of the sacred Muslim city of Mecca. There were several other pictures of Mecca, but we were very surprised that the crystal turned out looking exactly like one of them, one taken from the air. Also I found it almost frightening that the crystal possesses the exact atmosphere of the picture.

タイ　スカトー寺　３つの甕の雨水

Sukato Temple in Thailand・Rainwater from Three Jars

癒しの場と結晶の関係を調べる実験を行いました。タイにあるワッパ・スカトー寺 (Wat Pa Sukato) という瞑想をするためのお寺と、その周辺の森、さらにそこから離れた村に置かれた甕の雨水の結晶を調べました。甕に入った水は、雨季にふった雨水を甕に溜めたものです。恵みの雨は甕の置かれた場所によって、不思議な熟成の違いをみせてくれました。

We performed an experiment to investigate the relationship between places of healing and crystals. We checked crystals of rainwater contained in jars placed in the Wat Pa Sukato temple in Thailand, a temple for meditation, in the forest surrounding the temple, and in a village away from the temple. The water in the jar was rainwater collected during the rainy season. The blessed rain presented a puzzling difference in maturity depending on where it was kept.

村人の甕の雨水　　Rainwater from the jar in the village

村人の喜怒哀楽の感情を常に受けている場所ゆえ、気ぜわしさが水にも影響を与えたのでしょうか。３サンプル中、美しいものが１番少なかったのがこの甕の水でした。

Since the jar was in a place where it is constantly affected by the emotions of villagers, this restlessness may have influenced the water. Among three samples, the least number of beautiful crystals was found in this jar.

場を感じる

森の中の甕(かめ)の雨水　Rainwater from the jar in the forest

人の影響が1番少ない場所だけに、自然のリズムが雨水を育んだのでしょうか、村の甕の倍の美しい結晶を撮影できました。

Since it was the place with the least influence from people, the rhythms of nature may have nourished the rainwater. We were successful in obtaining double the number of beautiful crystals compared to the village.

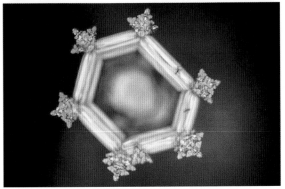

スカトー寺の甕の雨水

Rainwater from the jar in the temple

スカトー寺では日々、僧侶と信仰熱心な村人が瞑想をするそうです。癒しの空間は人びとの意識によってつくられるのでしょう。3サンプル中、もっともたくさんの美結晶が観察されました。

We heard that in the temple the priests and pious villagers meditate daily. A healing space has been created through the consciousness of the people. We observed the most number of beautiful crystals among the three samples.

場を感じる

象　Elephant

象、出雲大社、川古の大楠

Elephant, Izumo Shrine, Giant Camphor in Kawako

写真を水に見せてから結晶写真を撮ったところ、それぞれの写真の持つ特徴を見事にとらえた結晶が現れた例3点です。上の結晶写真には中央に象の鼻が見えますね。右ページ上では出雲大社の注連縄と、てっぺんに社の形が、右ページ下は大楠の入り組んだ根の形がそのまま写し出されています。この結果から、映像や形の持つ振動は、その形をそのままわたしたちの脳裏にとどめ置く、ということが考えられるかもしれません。念写や記憶のメカニズムを解明するカギといえるかもしれません。

We showed photographs to the water and took pictures of the crystals. These are three typical crystals that show the characteristics of the photographs. In the picture above, you can see the trunk of an elephant in the center of the crystal, in the picture right above, the shape of the Izumo Shrine sacred straw ropes and on the top the shape of the shrine, and the right below the exact shape of the complicated roots of a giant camphor tree has been projected. This result leads me to wonder if perhaps vibrations that are associated with images or shapes could perhaps remain in the brain in that form. This might perhaps be a clue to help us solve the mechanism of "thought photographs" and memory.

出雲大社　Izumo Shrine

川古の大楠　Giant Camphor in Kawako

第三章　言葉のちから

Chapter 3　　Power of Words

「はじめに言葉ありき」言葉はそれ自身がエネルギーです。
"In the Beginning, there was the Word":
words themselves are energy.

第三章　言葉のちから

「エネルギーとは振動であり、振動とは命でもある」と、わたしはいつもセミナーでいっています。そして「言葉は振動である」とも。ですから、3段論法でいえば「言葉は命でもある」わけです。

日本の古語においては、「言葉」の尊敬語は「命」と書いて、「みこと」といっていました。「みことば」の略と思われます。

日本の古語は、古神道がメインの文化のときに用いられていましたが、わたしは「神道」を信仰、あるいは宗教であるとは思っていません。神道は「しんとう」と現在では読みますが、昔は文字通り「しんどう」であったのではないかと思っています。

すなわち、「振動」が原義であったと思うのです。ということは、古代の日本人というか、大和人は「すべては振動からはじまる」「振動こそ命であり、光であり、音である」ことをわかっていて、それは神の道に通じるし、神そのものでもあると認識していたのだと思います。そう、今でいう量子力学をとっくの昔に究めていたのです。

言葉について、「なぜ、そこに力があるのか」「なぜ、言葉によって水の結晶が変化するのか」についても、言葉が振動であるからだと思うのです。

そもそも、言葉の起源とは何だったのでしょうか。わたしはそれを次のように考えています。

言葉は育てられた親から教えられるものです。もともとDNAの中には言葉の項目はないのです。

それでは、最初の人類はいったい何から言葉を教わったのでしょうか？

それは自然の振動・音からだと思います。自然はいろいろな音をだします。安全な音、危険な音、静かな音、うるさい音、愉快な音、不愉快な音、安心な音、不安になる音、不思議な音、ありふれた音、などです。

これらの音を聞き分けて仲間に伝える手段として、言葉はつくられたと思うのです。ですから、言葉の響きは自然の摂理そのものです。自然の摂理をデザイン化する水の結晶は、それがネガティブなときは結晶化せず、ポジティブなときには美しい6角形の結晶をつくるのです。

言葉がいろいろな国によって違うことも、この考え方で説明ができます。それぞれの国にはそれぞれの自然があります。言葉の基本となるべき自然の振動が違います。ですから、言葉は国というより風土によってわかれるわけです。しかし、自然の摂理はどこでも一緒ですから、たとえ言葉が違っても、その意味は同じになるのです。

水はどんな微細な振動をも伝えてくれる媒体です。たとえそれが発せられた言葉ではなく文字であっても、自然の振動として受け止め、結晶という形によって、そのエネルギーをわたしたちに見せてくれるのです。

まさに言葉は力を持っています。本章では良い言葉の数々の実験と、悪い言葉の少々の実験の結果をお見せします。過去、これらの言葉と密接なかたちで出合ったときのことを思い出しながら、もう1度それらの言葉の意味合いを、力を感じてみてください。

CHAPTER 3   Power of Words

In my seminars, I always stress that "energy is vibrations and vibrations are life". I follow this by saying, "words are vibrations". Syllogistically speaking, therefore, "words are life".

In archaic Japanese, the honorific term of "Kotoba(meaning words)"was written with the character, "命 ('Inochi' meaning life)" and pronounced as "Mikoto" which is presumed to be a shortened form of "Mikotoba (honorific term of words)" .

Archaic Japanese words were used during the times when ancient Shin-to was the main culture. I do not use "Shin-to" here to mean a cult or a religion. At present, the characters "神道" are pronounced as "Shin-to", but I believe that in the past it was literally pronounced as "Shin-do (meaning the Way of the Gods)".

In other words, I believe that "振動", read "Shin-do" (meaning "vibrations") was the original meaning "神道 ('Shin-do', meaning the Way of the Gods)".

That means the ancient Japanese or Yamato (Great Harmony) people knew that everything begins by vibrations. I believe that they were aware that "vibrations are life, light and sound", and that this led to the Way of the Gods or were the Gods themselves. They knew everything about what is now called quantum mechanics.

In regard to words, the answer to the questions, "Why do they have forces ?" and "Why do water crystals change depending on words?" is vibrations. After all how did words begin ? My idea is as follows:

Your parents, who raised you, taught you words. Words are not contained in DNA. How did the first human beings learn words ? I think that they learned from the vibrations in nature of which sounds are made up.

Various sounds can be heard in nature: safe sounds, dangerous sounds, quiet sounds, noisy sounds, pleasant sounds, unpleasant sounds, easy sounds, uneasy sounds, strange sounds, familiar sounds, and so on.

I think people created words for the purpose of distinguishing these sounds and sharing them with others. So the sounds of words are nothing less than a divine gift from nature. Water crystals illustrate in their design this divine gift of nature. Negatives prevent the water from crystallizing. Positives allow it to develop in beautiful hexagonal shapes.

This way of thinking provides a good reason for the differences in words around the world. Each country has its own unique natural environment. The vibrations in nature, which are the basis of words, therefore vary. Thus, words differ depending on the climate rather than the country. However, the gift of nature is the same everywhere, so although words can be different, the meaning is the same.

Water is a medium that receives and understands even the subtlest vibrations. Water captures vibrations naturally, even when they are in characters or letters representing language, and it shows us the energy they contain in the forms of crystals.

Words most certainly have forces. In this chapter, I will show you the results of a number of experiments with positive words and a few experiments with negative words. I would like you to remember a time when you encountered these words personally, and please feel, once again, the meaning and forces of these words.

家族愛　Family Love

「家族愛」という文字を見せた水の結晶です。昔は、家族は3代同居が普通でしたが、今や住宅事情や少子化によって、そうしたくてもできない家が多いですね。それによって、いろいろな問題がでているようです。水に「家族愛」の文字を見せたら、3代が重なったような結晶となりました。わたしには1番下が祖父母、真ん中が両親、手前が子どもたちのようにみえます。その中で、やはり祖父母の存在感が大事のような感じです。

Once it was common for three generations to live together as a family. In recent times this has become difficult because of housing conditions and the declining birthrate. This is creating various kinds of problems. When we showed the phrase "Fmily Love", the crystal grew into three layers. I interpret this as: the bottom layer represents the grandparents, the middle, the parents, and the top layer is the children. It gives the impression that the presence of the grandparents is the most important factor.

文字を見せる

隣人愛 Neighborly Love

「汝の隣人を愛せよ」とキリストはいいました。日本には「向こう三軒両隣」という言葉があります。互いに助け合いなさいという意味は同じですが、今やお隣さんとのお付き合いがまったくない人も多くなっているようです。この結晶を見て、もう1度、お隣さんを思いやりましょう。

Jesus said, "Love thy neighbor". There is a phrase in Japanese "three neighbors across and one on each side". Both mean the same to help one another. There seem to be many people nowadays who have no contact with their neighbors. Let's spare a thought once again for our neighbors while looking at this crystal.

祖国愛　Patriotism

後ろのぼんやりした大きな結晶は、それぞれの祖国でしょうか。わたしも国内にいるときは、
それほど祖国を意識しませんが、海外ではとても意識しています。日本人であることに誇り
を持ち、日本人であるからこその思いでお話しをし、人に会います。グローバル化の世の中、
もう祖国がどうのこうのといっておられませんよ、という人もいますが、まず自国を知り、
自国を愛することによって、他国を理解し、愛することができると思うのです。

The hazy large crystal in the back may represent one's homeland. I do not give much thought
to my homeland when I am at home, but I think a lot about it when abroad. I feel proud to be a
Japanese, and I meet and talk to people with that feeling because I am Japanese. Some people
might say that we need to grow beyond simple patriotism in order to achieve true globalization.
However, I believe we can only understand and love other countries when we know and love
ourselves.

文字を見せる

人類愛　　Love for Humanity

「隣人愛」ととてもよく似ている結晶です。やはり「部分は全体、全体は部分」を表わすのですね。まず、自分を愛することができて、家族を愛することができ、隣人を愛することができる。そして、隣人を愛することができて、祖国を愛し、人類を愛することができるのでしょう。

This crystal greatly resembles the one from "Neighborly Love". It truly expresses, after all, the idea "see a part to see the whole and see the whole to see a part", does it not ? First, you must be able to love yourself, and then you will be able to love your family. Only then can you love your neighbors, and from there, your homeland and mankind.

敬愛 Reverence

この結晶には、まさに「敬い愛するかたち」を見ることができます。わたしが最も敬愛するのは、今年102歳になる「正心調息法」という呼吸法を開発した医学博士　塩谷信男先生です。その方にお会いするときは、いつも自然に背筋がぴんとなり、その存在をいとおしむような姿勢になります。みなさんの敬愛する方を思い浮かべてください。きっとこの結晶のような感じをお持ちになるでしょう。

We can really see the "shape of love and respect" in this crystal. The person I most revere is Dr. Nobuo Shioya, who will be 102 years old this year (2003). He is a medical doctor who developed a method of breathing called Seishin-chousoku (method for correcting the mind and adjusting the breath). Whenever I see Dr. Shioya, I unconsciously assume an attitude of respect and find myself full of love and respect for his very existence. Please imagine a person you respect and love. I am sure you will have feelings that resemble this crystal.

文字を見せる

感動 Emotion

感動という言葉こそ振動の「共振現象」そのものです。感じて動かされる、ということは、ある物から何かを受けて振動することが、その人にとって最高のエネルギー源となるということです。ですから、1日に感動することが多ければ多いほど、元気な生活ができることになります。そして、「感動」という文字がつくりだす結晶にもまた、「祈りのかたち」がみえます。自分が願い祈っていたことに思いもかけず出合ったとき、人は感動するのでしょう。ポジティブな願いや祈りをたくさん持つことが、躍動的な生活を送る秘訣ではないでしょうか。

The word " 感動 (Kando)" is a resonance of vibrations. Kando literally means "to feel", "to be moved". To be affected by strong emotion by something and vibrate is the best energy source (energy and motion). The more Kando you have every day, the more energetic your life will be. Again, the crystals that were created from the word "Emotion (Kando)" have the "shape of prayer". When you accidentally encounter something you have been hoping and praying for, you feel a thrill. This should give you a clue for how to live a vibrant life, should it not？ Having a lot of positive desires and praying for them is the key to living a richly emotional life, I believe.

絶望　Despair

やはり大方は、いじけて無残な結晶となっていましたが、1つ2つ、6角形にはなってはいないものの、この結晶のように、何とか立ち直って美しくなるんだ、という思いを感じさせるものがありました。そうですね、絶望は新しい希望へのスタートと思いましょう。

As expected, most crystals developed timidly and turned out pitiful. On the other hand, there were one or two crystals similar to this one that did not quite form a hexagon. We can feel their desire to work vigorously to recover and grow beautiful. Let us realize here that despair may be the start of new hope !

文字を見せる

希望　Hope

この「希望」の結晶は、本来は映像でお見せしたかったものです。というのは、見事にバランスのとれた6つの枝葉が伸びてゆくさまを見るだけで、希望を持つことは、素晴らしいことだと実感できるからです。そして、結晶がこのようにすくすくと成長してゆくとき、そのコアはとてもしっかりしたものになっています。基礎をしっかりした上でこそ大きな希望が持てるのですね。

This is the crystal for "Hope". We actually wanted to show this through video, as by watching the six well balanced branches grow, you would definitely feel that having hope is wonderful. In addition, when crystals grow and thrive in this manner, the core is constructed strongly. Only when provided with a solid foundation can great hope thrive.

水は答えを教えてくれました…

The water taught us…

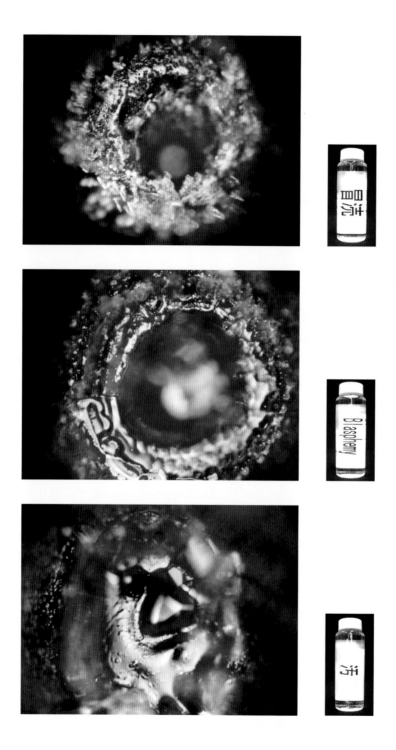

冒涜 Blasphemy

<ruby>冒<rt>ぼ</rt></ruby><ruby>涜<rt>う</rt></ruby>とく

冒涜とは、神聖・尊厳なるものを犯し汚すこと、という意味で、「神を冒
涜する者」などと使います。そして、この字をよくみると、「涜」という
字は「さんずい」に「売る」と書きますから「水を売る」という意味です。「水
は神の遣い」かもしれない、というわたしの仮説を裏づけるもので、はじ
めてこれに気づいたときには鳥肌が立ちました。また、日本語、英語とも
同じような結晶になったのも象徴的です。しかし、今は水を売るのは致し
かたないことです。過去において、わたしたちは水を相当汚してしまいま
したから。将来はこの意味合いを良く考えて、「水はみんなで分かち合う
もの」としていきたいですね。

Blasphemy

Blasphemy is a contemptuous or profane act, utterance, or writing concerning
God or a sacred entity. When you look at the composition of the characters
carefully, " 涜 " is composed with the "water" radical on the left-hand side,
"Uru", which means "to sell", on the right-hand side, giving us the meaning of
"to sell water". This supports my hypothesis that "water may be a messenger
of God". When I thought this for the first time I got goose bumps. It is also
symbolic that from both Japanese and English we obtained the same type of
crystals. Throughout recent history, we have seriously polluted our water.
This can explain the reason why we have to sell and buy water. Reflecting on
this for the future, I would like us to be able to live in a world where "water is
something we all respect and share".

汚 Filth

汚という字の右側のつくりの部分は溝の意味だそうです。溝に水がたまる、
すなわち淀むと水は汚れますが、「汚」の字を水に見せたところ、女の子
の顔に、めちゃめちゃな落書きがされたような結晶になってしまいました。
こんな字を使わなくてすむ世の中にしたいものです。

I have heard that the right part of the character " 汚 " means ditch. The left part
means water. When water pools in a ditch, it gets filthy and stagnates. We
showed this word to the water, and a crystal appeared showing a girl's face
covered with terrible graffiti. I wish we could make a world where such a word
does not have to be used.

Human Cloning（クローン人間）

水はこの文字に対してはっきりと「ノー」といいました。自然ではないからでしょう。おまけに中央の石版のようなものには、不気味な暗号が書かれているかのようです。何でしょうこの暗号は認識票かな？

The water firmly said, "No !" to this word. It's probably because it is not natural. In addition to that, there appears to be a strange code on something that looks like a slate palette in the middle. What does this intriguing code mean ? Is it some sort of identification ?

文字を見せる

真理 Truth

完璧なシンメトリー（左右対称）ですね。ヨーロッパでは幾何学模様（ジオメトリー）の中にこそ真理がある、という人が多いのですが、まさにそのような感じです。真理（子）さんという名前は、日本人にはとても多いのですが、この結晶を見て喜ばれると思います。いつも眺めていたい、机の上に置いておきたい、そんな結晶です。

This crystal has perfect symmetry. Many people in Europe say that in geometry lies truth. This actually gives me this impression. 真 理 is pronounced "Shinri" meaning "truth", and also pronounced "Mari" when used as a woman's name. Both Mari and Mariko are very common female names among Japanese, and I am sure that they would be very pleased to see this crystal. It is a crystal that beckons us to admire it all the time and keep it on our desk.

永遠　Eternity

完璧なシンメトリーの形状で、一見、2重構造のように見えます。撮影者は1番外枠の結晶にフォーカスをしていますから、中枠の結晶はぼやけています。そして、もちろん1番中側のコアも。しかし、それぞれに同時にフォーカスすることができていたら、まったく相似の結晶が撮れていたに違いありません。そして、顕微鏡の倍率をどんどん高めていったとき、それこそ永遠に同じ形のものが確認できたのではないでしょうか。

This crystal also possesses perfect symmetry, and at first glance it looks like it has an overlapping structure. The photographer focused on the outermost part of the crystal, leaving the inner core of the crystal blurred. I believe if we had been able to focus on each part at the same time we would have seen crystals of perfect conformity in shape. Then, if we increased the magnification of the microscope still higher, we would have seen never-ending crystals of the same shape.

文字を見せる

愛 感謝　Love and Thanks

「愛 感謝」の結晶を得て、わたしの宇宙観は変わりました。過去から現在に至るまで撮影された結晶の中で、いちばん美しい結晶をつくった「愛 感謝」の概念こそが、この宇宙の概念だったのだ、神の意思だったのだと、悟らされたのです。「愛」というアクティブなエネルギーと、「感謝」というパッシブなエネルギーとが共鳴して、この宇宙がつくられたという、真に清く深い宇宙観を、わたしは教えられたのです。

Obtaining the crystal of "Love and Thanks" changed my vision of the cosmos. I realized that the concept of "Love and Thanks" created the most beautiful crystal among those taken to this date. The concept of "Love and Thanks" is the concept of the universe, or perhaps God's benevolent intention. I was shown, in a real, pure and profound vision of the cosmos, that the active energy of "love" and the passive energy of "thanks" resonate together, and that this is how the universe was created.

水の答えは「イエス」それとも「ノー」？

Is the answer from the water "Yes" or "No"?

麻 Hemp

麻はこれからの人類にとって、たいへん有用な植物であるとわたしは信じていますが、ただ１つ、麻薬物質が抽出できるために、現在は地球規模で排斥されています。水に聞いてみました。左は「大麻」の写真を右は「麻」の文字を見せた結晶ですが、水もわたしの意見に「イエス」といってくれました。

麻、大麻 古来より世界各地に自生し、人びとの生活文化に役立てられてきた大麻。その利用価値が認められ、さまざまな分野での産業利用が試みられている。

麻　Hemp

I believe that hemp (cannabis) is a very valuable plant. Due to the fact that hemp rope and marijuana come from the same plant, its cultivation is currently against the law in most of the world. We showed the word for "Hemp" to the water. The left crystal is from the picture of hemp and the right crystal is from the Japanese word for hemp. In my opinion, the water crystals replied in the affirmative for man's use of hemp.

Hemp　　Hemp has been grown naturally since ancient times and has been positively used to enhance people's life and culture. Its value has been recognized and industrial use is progressing in various fields.

第四章　祈りのちから

Chapter 4　　Power of a Prayer

もしも、世界の人びとが一緒に祈ったら……。
If the people of the world prayed to water….

第四章　祈りのちから

　1970年4月11日に打ち上げられた、アポロ13号の奇跡の地球帰還のことについては、数年前に映画もつくられて、全世界で新たなる感動を呼びましたから、ご存知の方も多いと思います。

　あのとき、地球に無事に帰還できる割合は300万分の1ぐらいであったとも、後にいわれましたが、なぜそのような確率で、あの3人の宇宙飛行士の奇跡の生還はありえたのでしょうか。

　わたしは当時27歳でしたが、このときの一部始終は、テレビでも中継で流していましたから、それを深夜遅くまで見ていて良く覚えています。

　そして、わたしにとって真剣に祈ったという経験は、今から考えてみると、このときがはじめてであったように思います。画面を見ながら、地上と3人の宇宙飛行士とのやり取りを聞きながら、手に汗をし、身を乗り出してテレビの画面をじっと凝視し、まるで自分が3人の飛行士の家族のような感覚で、ただひたすら無事に帰還できるよう、純粋に祈っていました。

　その手はいつの間にか合わされて、「祈りのかたち」となっていたように思います。

　テレビは同時に世界各地の人びとが、彼らの無事を願って祈っているさまを映しだしていました。それはバチカンでのローマ法王の祈り、エルサレム嘆きの壁でのユダヤ教徒たちの祈り、不確かな記憶ですが、アジアのどこかでの黄色い僧衣をまとった仏教徒たちの祈り、アラブにおける

イスラム教徒たちの祈り、そして、もちろん一般市民の祈りと、宗教・宗派を超えて、世界中の人びとが3人の無事を願って祈っているさまがそこにありました。

　今から思えば、世界の人びとが同じ願いを持って祈ったのは、あのときがはじめてではなかったでしょうか。そうです。あのときは世界中の人の心が1つになっていました。アメリカ人もヨーロッパ人もユダヤ人もアラブ人もアジア人もありませんでした。すなわち世界人類皆兄弟、みんながブラザー・アンド・シスターでした。だからこそあの奇跡は成し遂げられたのだと、わたしは強く信じています。

　「祈りのちから」、それは何に対してどのように作用するのでしょうか？ わたしにはまだ、そのすべてのメカニズムを説明することはできません。

　ただ1つ自信を持っていえることは、水に対して働きかけ、それが通じたときに、水の構造を変えることができるということです。そして、きっとそれは、願いを叶えてくれる物理的エネルギーに変換されるのでしょう。

　水に対しての祈りの実験を数多く行い、結晶が確実に美しく変化する結果を得て、わたしはそのことを確信するにいたったのです。

　本章では、「祈り」の前後の水の結晶の変化をご紹介することといたします。

CHAPTER 4   The Power of Prayer

Many people know of the Apollo 13 space launch in April 1970 and its miraculous return to Earth. The movie "Apollo 13" was produced several years ago and it revived this adventure to the entire world. It was later estimated that their safe return to Earth had a chance of one in three million. How could the astronauts possibly have returned successfully against such tremendous odds?

I was 27 years old at the time, and I remember clearly watching it on TV until late at night. The TV stations were broadcasting all of the details. Thinking back on it now, I believe that for the first time in my life I prayed hard. I was watching the screen and listening to the exchanges between the ground crew on Earth and the three astronauts. My hands were sweaty and I was leaning forward, my eyes fixed on the screen. I felt similar to how the families of the three astronauts must have. My whole being was praying for their safe return. My hands were, without my knowledge, together in the "shape of prayer".

At the same time, the TV was showing scenes of people the world over praying for their safe return. The prayers of the Pope in the Vatican, of the Jews at the Wailing Wall in Jerusalem, and, if memory serves, the prayers of Buddhists in yellow garb somewhere in Asia, of the Muslims in Arabia, and of course the prayers of society in general.

There were scenes of the entire global community praying for the safety of these three astronauts. Neither religion nor sect limited the desire of the world for their safe return.

Looking back now, this might perhaps have been the first time that the people of the world prayed for the same thing. The heart of the global community was indeed as one at that time. There was no difference between Americans, Europeans, Jews, Arabs, or Asians. Everyone was brother and sister. I firmly believe that was how the miracle of the astronauts' safe return was made possible.

How can we know how the power of prayer works? I cannot explain the mechanism at this time. The only one thing that I can say with confidence is that when it works in the water, and the water is affected, then it can change its structure. This, in and of itself, changes the physical energy in accordance with the wish. I have been convinced of this after carrying out many experiments in praying to water with the results that the crystals are clearly transformed to become more beautiful. This chapter introduces the structure of water crystals before and after the "prayer" to examine how they have transformed.

藤原ダムの水に加持祈祷

Incantations and Prayers to the Water of Fujiwara Dam

　真言密教の行者、加藤宝喜住職による1時間の加持祈祷後の水の結晶の変化です。加持祈祷とは火を燃やしながら仏さまと一体となって、印を結び願いごとと共に経を唱える、という弘法大師直伝の行です。

　この実験は1997年10月群馬県の藤原ダムで行われました。わたしもこのとき立ち会ったのですが、「祈りのちから」を目の前でまざまざと見せられたはじめての体験でした。くわしくは140ページで述べさせていただきますが、ごらんのように祈祷前の結晶と、その後の結晶の神がかり的な美醜の差、これがなぜ起こったのか、その謎を解くのに5年必要としました。

　ここでは右ページのこの世のものとは思えない、幻想的な芸術をじっくりとご鑑賞ください。

　This is how the water crystal changed after an hour incantations by Hoki Kato, an ascetic priest of Shingon Tantric Buddhism. The "Kaji" prayer is a service directly transmitted from the ancient priest Kobo Daishi, and involves the light of the Buddha reflecting on the water of the soul, making the supplicant and the Buddha as one. The wish is recited along with the sutra as a fire burns.

　This experiment was conducted at Fujiwara Dam in Gunma Prefecture in October 1997. I witnessed it myself, and it was my first experience in seeing clearly the "power of prayer". You can see deity's work in the difference between the crystal's appearance and beauty before and after the incantations. It took me five years to discover the mystery of why this happened.

　The details are described on page 140. I hope you will enjoy the magical art of heavenly beauty as presented on the left page.

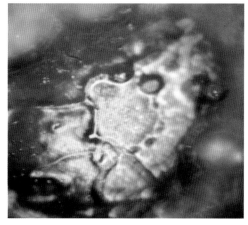

ダムの水　加持祈祷前
Dam water　Before the incantations and prayers

ダムの水　加持祈祷後
Dam water　After the incantations and prayers

7角形の結晶も現れました。
A heptagonal crystal appeared as well.

ダムの水　加持祈祷後
Dam water　After the incantations and prayers

ビデオ「水からの伝言」　親子の水への祈り

The Experiment of Prayer from the Video *The Message from Water*

　2002年10月、わたしたちは実際に成長する美しい結晶を、何とか「水からの伝言」の読者にお見せしたいと思い、ビデオを制作し、見事に成功しました。その中で1番の冒険だったのが祈りの実験の企画です。すべてをリアルタイムで行わなければ説得力がありません。4組の親子に参加していただき、普段は絶対に結晶をつくらない東京の水道水に短い祈り（3分）を捧げてもらいました。そして3時間それを凍らせた後、参加者がテレビモニターで観察する中で結晶撮影が行われました。子どもたちと親たちの純粋な祈りのエネルギーは、右ページの写真のように水に見事に通じたのです。

　Having decided we would like to show the actual growing of beautiful crystals to the readers of *The Message from Water*, we succeeded in capturing this on video in October 2002. Among the most adventurous was a project of prayer experimentation where everything had to be done in real time in order to be convincing. We had four pairs of parents and children. They each gave a short prayer (three minutes) to the tap water of Tokyo, which usually never forms crystals. Then, after freezing it for three hours, we videotaped the crystals while the participants were watching via a TV monitor. The energy of pure prayer from the children and the parents was conveyed beautifully, as you can see in the picture on the right.

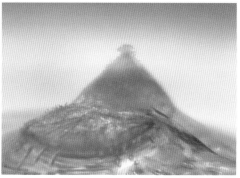

東京浅草橋の水道水、祈り後
The tap water of Asakusabashi, Tokyo   After the prayer

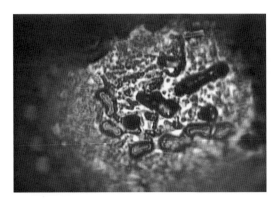

東京浅草橋の水道水、祈り前
The tap water of Asakusabashi, Tokyo   Before the prayer

ブラジル　カラピクイバの湖での水への祈り
The Ceremony of Prayer at a Lake in Carapicuiba, Brazil.

　2002 年 11 月、わたしは訪問先のサンパウロで、地元の NGO 団体のメンバーと共に、ひどい汚染で問題になっていたカラピクイバの湖の岸辺に立ち、祈りによる水の浄化セレモニーを行いました。下の写真でおわかりのように、参加者がそれほど多くはなかったため、わたしは湖の水に直接向かって祈ることをやめ、ペットボトルにその湖の水を入れて、その周りを全員で手をつないで、いつものように祈りました。

　その結果、左ページの祈りの前の水の結晶に対して、右ページのように、ペットボトルに入れた水だけでなく、祈りの後の湖の水も美しく変化したのです。「部分は全体、全体は部分」という相似理論が証明されたのです。

　In November 2002, I was visiting San Paulo, Brazil. I stood with the local NGO members near the bank of a lake in Carapicuiba. The lake was terribly polluted. We performed a water purification ceremony through prayer. As you see in the picture below, we were a small group. Therefore, instead of praying to the lake water directly, we held hands as we stood around and prayed over a plastic bottle of the lake water.

　As a result, the water crystals before the prayer changed to the beautiful ones on the right. Not only did the water in the plastic bottle change, but so did the water of the lake, as its crystals became more beautiful after the prayer. The similarity theory of "the part is also the whole; the whole is also the part" was verified.

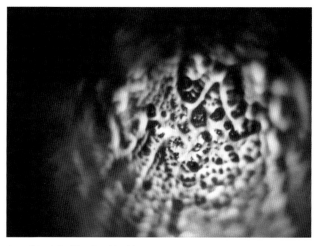

カラピクイバの湖の水　祈り前
The water of a lake in Carapicuiba　Before the prayer

祈りの輪の中心に置いたペットボトルに入れたカラピクイバの湖の水　祈り後
The water of a lake in Carapicuiba placed in the center of the prayer circle　After the prayer

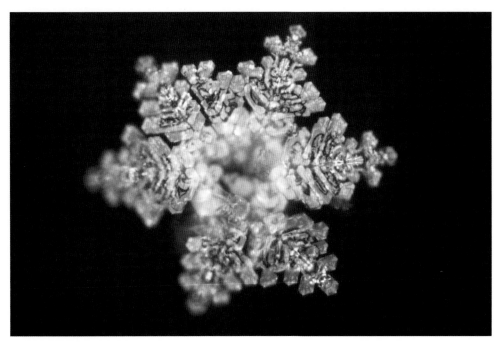

カラピクイバの湖の水　祈り後
The water of a lake in Carapicuiba　After the prayer

世界の水に、愛と感謝の思いを伝えよう
Let's Give Our Love and Thanks to the Water of the World

　2003 年 7 月 25 日の夜明け、わたしはキリストゆかりの湖、イスラエルのガリラヤ湖畔におよそ 200 人の仲間と共にたたずみ、「水への愛と感謝プロジェクト」の提唱者として、敬虔なる愛と感謝の祈りをガリラヤ湖の水に捧げました。

　同日、世界の 33 カ国、100 あまりのチームが、それぞれの水辺で同じように愛と感謝の祈りを、それぞれの水に対して捧げたのです。

　この 1 年間、わたしがその国を訪れて直接声を掛けた人たち、同プロジェクトのホームページを見て賛同した人たちが参加してくれたのです。

　このプロジェクトは、2000 年 3 月から世界各地を講演旅行のために回るようになったわたしが、いろいろな国の人たちの平和に対する切実なる思いを肌で感じるようになり、何とかしてその思いを具現化したいと願って立ち上げたものです。その中からいくつかの結果報告をさせていただきたいと思います。

At dawn on July 25, 2003 I stood with 200 fellow members by Lake Galilee in Israel, the lake that is famed for its connection with Jesus Christ, and offered a prayer of devout love and thanks to the water of lake in my capacity as the proponent of "Project of Love and Thanks to Water".

On the same day, about 100 teams in 33 countries in the world offered the prayer of love and thanks by their waters in the same way.

The participants in the prayers were both people I directly contacted during my visit to those countries in the past year and those supporters who read our homepage.

I launched this project with the desire to make real the earnest hopes for peace that I felt directly when I travelled throughout the world from March 2000 to give my lectures. Let me tell you about some of the results.

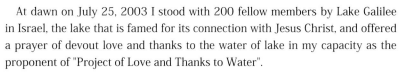

イスラエル　ガリラヤから東京への祈り

The Prayer from Galilee to Tokyo

7月25日の「水への愛と感謝プロジェクト」前夜祭で、わたしが講演したセミナー会場から、参加者約200名に、東京のわたしのオフィスにあらかじめ置かれている水道水に対して、祈りを送ってもらいました。普段はけっして結晶をつくることのない東京の水道水が、ごらんのようにきれいな結晶をつくったのです（144頁参照）。人の祈りは距離に関係なく届くという1つの例です。

On the evening before the "Project of Love and Thanks to Water", we asked the 200 participants in my seminar to send prayers from the seminar venue of my lecture to the tap water prepared beforehand and standing in my office in Tokyo. The tap water of Tokyo, which normally never crystallizes, made a beautiful crystal as you can see on page 144.

水に祈る　Prayers to Water

ドイツ　ダイニンゲル ヴァイヘル湖
Lake Deiniger Weiher, Germany

　ドイツ　ミュンヘン郊外の森の中にある美しい湖。家族や恋人たちの憩いの場として親しまれているようで、子どもたちの歓声や鳥のさえずりが心地良い所です。

　ホームページなどの呼びかけに賛同して集まった約250名が午後7時半から、水に愛と感謝の祈りを捧げました。

Wasser, wir lieben Dich	（お水さん　愛しています）
Wasser, wir danken Dir	（お水さん　ありがとう）
Wasser, wir respektieren Dich	（お水さん　尊敬しています）

ダイニンゲル　ヴァイヘル湖の水
祈り前

The water of Lake Deiniger Weiher
Before the prayer

A beautiful lake in the forest near Munich, Germany, a place with birdsong and children's shouts of joy, perfect for recreation and relaxation for families and lovers. About 250 supporters, many of whom had answered the call on my homepage gathered at 7:30 in the evening and offered the prayer of love and thanks to the water.

Wasser, wir lieben Dich	(Water, we love you)
Wasser, wir danken Dir	(Water, we thank you)
Wasser, wir respektieren Dich	(Water, we respect you)

もともと汚染度の少ない湖なのでしょう、かわいい結晶が撮れています。

Perhaps due to low levels of contaminants in the lake originally, we have managed to create a lovely crystal.

ダイニンゲル　ヴァイヘル湖の水　祈り後　　The water of Lake Deiniger Weiher　　After the prayer

同じ倍率で撮影しているのですが、空路送られてきた水にもかかわらず、とても大きい結晶となりました。つまりエネルギーをたくさん受けているといえます。

The magnification was the same, but a large crystal appeared. We can say that that means a lot of energy had been received.

韓国 全羅北道 扶安ダム

Buan Dam, Jeollabuk-do, Korea

　７月２５日の「水への愛と感謝プロジェクト」にあわせて、韓国、扶安ダムでは、子どもたちが童謡発表をしたり、結晶写真を印刷した紙で折った船を流したりと、とても有意義な行事が行われました。このようなセレモニーが毎年行われることを願っています。

　「水」はわたしたちに「愛と感謝」を教え、実践させるようにする哲学であり、生活そのものでもあり、友だちでもあります。

On the same day, July 25, as the "Project of Love and Thanks to Water", a very meaningful event was held at Buan Dam in Korea. There were presentations of children's songs by the children, and the floating of folded paper boats printed with crystal pictures. I hope this kind of ceremony will be held every year. "Water" is a philosophy that teaches us "Love and Thanks" and helps us to achieve it; it is our life as well as our friend.

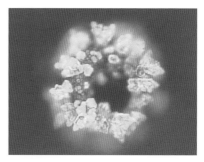

扶安ダムの水　祈り前
The water of Buan Dam　Before the praying

かろうじてリング状の結晶が１つありました。
We were lucky to get just one ring-shaped crystal.

扶安ダムの水　祈り後　　The water of Buan Dam　After the praying
力強い６角形の結晶に変化しました。
It turned into a powerful hexagonal crystal.

琵琶湖
Lake Biwa

　1999年の琵琶湖での成果（142頁）はわたしたちに大きな自信と勇気を与えてくれました。

　4年後の2003年7月25日、天気は曇り。日本の子宮といわれる琵琶湖から世界の水に向けて、愛と感謝の祈りのエネルギーを発信しました。

　当日、琵琶湖全体を囲むことはできませんでしたが、北部に浮かぶ竹生島(ちくぶ)をはじめ、今津、近江舞子(おうみまいこ)、大津、近江八幡(おおみはちまん)と湖の周囲6点で六角形をつくりセレモニーを行いました。

　採水はセレモニーの前日7月23日と終了後の7月25日深夜に行われ、さらには1ヵ月後の8月25日にも行いました。

　The result of the Lake Biwa event in 1999 (page 142) gave us great confidence and encouragement.

　The weather of July 25, 2003 was cloudy. The energy of the love and thanks prayer was sent out from Lake Biwa, called "the womb of Japan", to the world.

　Though it was not possible to surround the lake in order to conduct the ceremony, we were able to make a hexagon, positioning ourselves at six points: Chikubu island in the north, and Imazu, Omi-maiko, Otsu, and Omi-hachiman on the banks.

　The water was sampled on July 23 before the ceremony and again after the ceremony on July 25 late at night, and again a month later, on August 25.

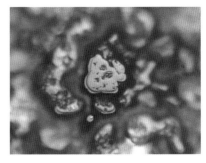

琵琶湖の水　祈り前
The water of Lake Biwa Before the prayer

残念ながら琵琶湖の汚染はまだまだ続いているようです。

Unfortunately Lake Biwa is still contaminated.

琵琶湖の水　祈り後
The water of Lake Biwa　After the prayer

琵琶湖の水　祈り1ヵ月後
The water of Lake Biwa　A month after the prayer

原形とは比較にならないほど美しい6角形の結晶、そして中には高い次元を示すものと思われる7角形の結晶も見つかりました。

We achieved a hexagonal crystal that was incomparably more beautiful than the original form, and even a heptagonal crystal that is thought to be showing a higher dimension.

広島平和記念公園

Hiroshima Peace Memorial Park

　7月25日の朝に広島市の中心地でもある原爆ドーム前の元安川の河川敷に10名の方が集まり、平和公園内の「平和の灯」がある池の水を採取して、全員で手をつなぎ、水への感謝、平和への祈りを捧げました。祈りの間は変化がなかったのですが、水への祈りを終えた途端に、大雨が降ってきました。

　雨もわたしたちにエールを送ってくれたのでしょう。感謝、感謝でした。

In the morning of July 25, 10 people gathered at the riverbed of the Motoyasu river in front of the skeletal remains that is the monument to the atomic bombing in the center of Hiroshima City. The people held hands one another and offered the prayer of thanks and peace to the water which was taken from the pond of the "Flame of Peace" in the Peace Park. Nothing changed during the prayer, but the moment the prayer ended, a very heavy rain started.

The rain sent us cheers as well. I was overwhelmed with thankfulness.

平和記念公園の噴水（水道水）　祈り前
The tap water of Hiroshima Peace Memorial Park　Before the prayer

おそらく下水道水を循環しているのでしょう。きれいな結晶は見つかりませんでした。

It is perhaps circulated sewer water. We could not find beautiful crystals.

平和記念公園の噴水（水道水）　祈り後
The tap water of Hiroshima Peace Memorial Park　After the prayer

「祈りのかたち」がはっきりと出ています。もう少し人数が多ければさらに完璧な形となっていたでしょう。
A clear "shape of prayer" appeared. If we had had a few more people with us, the shape would have grown more perfect.

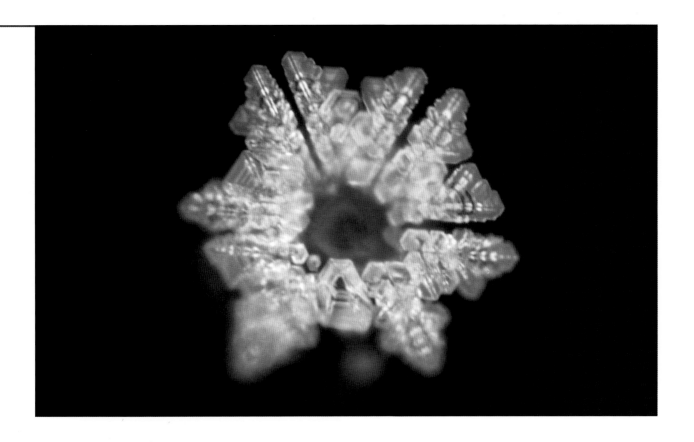

7月25日 希釈統合水　July 25 Diluted Mixed

　世界から、あるいは国内から送られてきた、約30種類の愛と感謝の捧げられた水を1つにしました。ミネラル分が多いものもありましたので、それを蒸留水で1000倍に希釈した水の結晶です。「合掌」の結晶（20頁）とよく似ています。各地でみなさんが心を込めて祈った結果が「祈りのかたち」となって表わされたようです。

　We mixed about thirty kinds of water sent from various places in Japan and overseas, to which had been offered the prayer of love and thanks. Since some of the water had a large volume of minerals, we diluted it with distilled water by a thousand to get crystals. This looks similar to the crystal of "Gassho (hands joined in prayer)" (page 20). It seems that the results of everyone's prayer from their heart in each part of the world appeared as the "shape of prayer".

韓国　円寂寺

Won-jok Temple, Korea

　韓国にある寺、円寂寺には山からの清水を汲む水場があります。ここでは毎日尼僧たちが水への感謝の祈りを捧げながら水を汲んでいます。常日頃から感謝の祈りを捧げているこの場所には、すでに「感謝の場」が出来上がっているようです。
　元水である山の清水からは完璧な結晶が得られなかったのに対して、水場の水からは祈りのエネルギーが凝縮したような美しい結晶が現れました。

There is a place in Won-jok Temple, a convent in Korea, where spring water from the mountain is drawn by nuns who pray here daily. This is a place where prayers of thanks are offered all the time, and it seems that a "place of thanks" has been constructed.

While no crystals were obtained from the mountain spring water, from the water of this "thanks" place a beautiful crystal, like the condensation of the energy of prayer, was formed.

円寂寺の水　祈り前
The water of Won-jok Temple　Before the prayer

116

円寂寺の水　祈り後
The water of Won-jok Temple　After the prayer

小学校の児童による
渡良瀬遊水地と水道水に声かけ実験

The Experiment with the Water of Watarase Drainage Basin and Tap Water by Primary School Students

『水からの伝言』が話題になった小学校で、結晶映像のスライドを見せながらセミナーを行いました。セミナーを通じて子どもたちには、言葉や気持ちが水に伝わることを良く理解してもらえたようです。

　セミナーの最後に「悪い言葉は使わないように気をつける人は手をあげてください」との問いかけに、ほぼ子どもたち全員が元気に「はーい」と答えてくれました。そして、子どもたちや先生方にも協力してもらい、水への祈りの実験を教室で行いました。実験は大成功でした。

　子どもたちの純粋な思いは水にたしかに伝わったのです。

In a primary school where The *Message from Water* became a topic of conversation, I gave a seminar showing my slides of crystal pictures. Through the seminar, the children seemed to have understood that language and feelings can be conveyed to the water.

To the request I made at the end of the talk, "please raise your hand if you are going to be careful not to use bad language", almost all the children answered positively. After the seminar, with the support of the children and the teachers, we conducted an experiment of praying to water in the classroom. The experiment was a great success.

The children's pure feelings were clearly conveyed to the water.

小学校水道水、祈り前
The tap water from a primary school　　Before the prayer

渡良瀬遊水地の水、祈り前
The water of Watarase drainage basin　　Before the prayer

小学校の水道水、祈り後
The tap water from a primary school   After the prayer

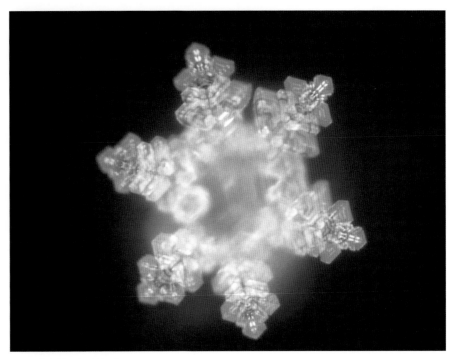

渡良瀬遊水地の水、祈り後
The water of Watarase drainage basin   After the prayer

ある町の水道水
The Change of Some Tap Water

　ある町からセミナーに呼ばれて、あらかじめその町の水道水を送ってもらい、その結晶を撮りました。ごらんのようにかなりひどい結晶です。そのままお見せしてはもうしわけないと思い、同じ水に1つには「愛」、もう1つには「愛感謝」という文字を貼ったところ、水はみごとに蘇りました。

　I was asked to give a seminar for a town in Japan. I asked them to send a sample of their tap water beforehand, and took a picture of a crystal. As you can see, it was pretty bad. Feeling embarrassed about having to show it like that, we took pictures of the same water, this time after attaching the character "Love" to one and "Love and Thanks" to the other. The water revived beautifully.

ある町の水道水に「愛」の文字を見せた後
After showing the word "Love" to the tap water of a town

ある町の水道水に「愛 感謝」の文字を見せた後
After showing the word "Love and Thanks" to the tap water of a town

重症急性呼吸器症候群の文字を見せる
その水に、「愛 感謝」の文字を見せると……

We showed the word "SARS", which means "Severe Acute Respiratory Syndrome"
When we showed that water the words "Love and Thanks", ……

　昨年の冬「サーズ」が流行っていたときです。わたしは思いたって、「SARS」と「サーズ」の文字を水に見せて結晶を撮ってほしいとスタッフに依頼しました。

　結果は、普段の蒸留水の結晶とほとんど変わりがありませんでした。「ふむ、そうか」としばらく考えたわたしは、サーズという略語ではなく、正式な病名「重症急性呼吸器症候群」とタイプを打たせて、もう1度テストをしてもらいました。結果はごらんのように、普段いくつかは良い結晶がでる蒸留水なのですが、全滅となりました（右上）。　やはり略語の場合、ある程度の期間それが定着しないと、水は認識ができないようです。

　次にわたしはそのビンに半分ほど残った水をそのまま残して、貼ってあったラベルを剥がして「愛 感謝」と書いたラベルに貼り替えました。そして1日たってまたその水を撮影してもらったのです。その結果が次の写真です（124頁）。ごらんのようにみんな美しい写真に復活したのです。蘇生したともいえます。

　さらに念のため、今度は英語で同じことをやってみました。「Severe Acute Respiratory Syndrome」を貼った結果です（右下）。それを剥がして「Love & Thanks」に貼り替えた結果です（125頁）。日本語でも英語でもまったく同じような結果となりました。

　この実験からわたしは次のような確信や新たなる考察を得るにいたりました。

① 水は的確に文字の振動を感じ、それに対して結晶的に反応する。
② 日本語でも英語でもその言葉が正しく使われていれば反応は同じである。
③ 文字の情報はできるだけ詳細の方が良い。
④ 「愛 感謝」の文字は大変ポジティブなエネルギーがある。
⑤ 水はたとえ1度だめになっても、良い環境にあえれば、再び良いエネルギーを持つ水となり得る（蘇生できる）。

　人はほとんど水でできています。
　ですから、わたしたちも上に述べたような物理的性質を持っているわけです。
　そう理解できれば、人生なかなか捨てたものでもありませんね。

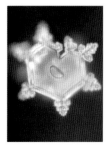

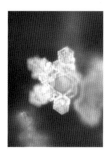

実験の元となる蒸留水の結晶
Crystals of distilled water that form
the basis of the experiment

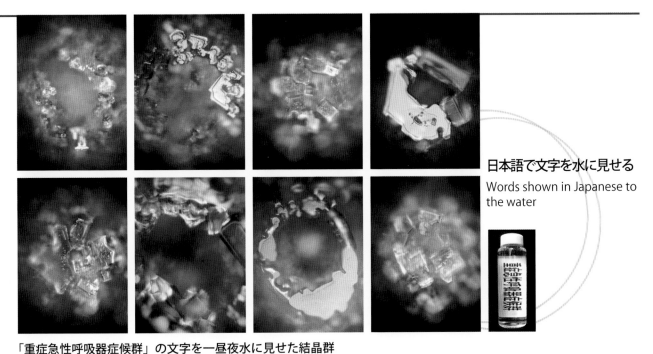

日本語で文字を水に見せる
Words shown in Japanese to the water

「重症急性呼吸器症候群」の文字を一昼夜水に見せた結晶群
A series of crystals which were achieved by showing the word "jusho-kyusei-kokyuki-shokogun" (Severe Acute Respiratory Syndrome) for a whole day and night

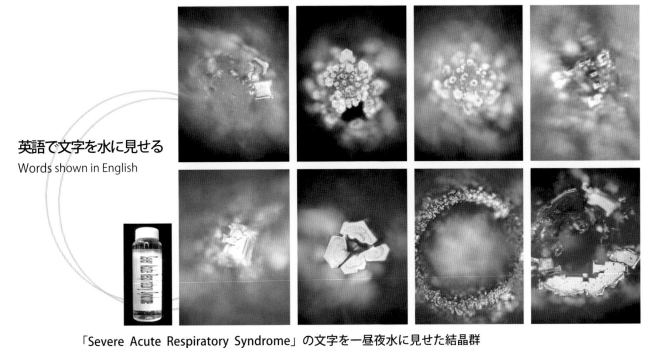

英語で文字を水に見せる
Words shown in English

「Severe Acute Respiratory Syndrome」の文字を一昼夜水に見せた結晶群
A series of crystals which were achieved by showing the word "Severe Acute Respiratory Syndrome" for a whole day and night

日本語「愛 感謝」の文字に貼りかえて水に見せる
Water shown the replacement label with the words "Love and Thanks" in Japanese

「重症急性呼吸器症候群」を見せた水に「愛 感謝」と貼りかえ、一昼夜水に見せた後の結晶群
A series of crystals gained after showing the replaced label "ai kansha" (Love and Thanks)" to the water which had shown "jusho-kyusei-kokyuki-shokogun" (Severe Acute Respiratory Syndrome).

We showed the word "SARS", which means "Severe Acute Respiratory Syndrome" When we showed that water the words "Love and Thanks", ……

This was when "SARS" was prevalent last winter. I had an idea to ask the staff to show "SARS" and "SARS" in Japanese to the water and to take pictures of the crystals.

The results did not have much difference from the crystals of normal distilled water. I thought about it a while, and then I asked them this time to type the name of the syndrome fully, instead of the abbreviation "SARS", and test again. The result was, as you see, that none of them crystallized well, though distilled water normally provides some good crystals (page 123). As expected, an abbreviated word needs some time to settle to enable the water to recognize it.

Next I left the half remaining water in the bottle and pealed the label off to replace it with the label written as "Love & Thanks". After a day, I asked them to take pictures of the water again. The result is the following pictures (page 124). As you can see, the crystals all revived to create beautiful pictures. We could say they were restored.

In order to make sure, we tried the same thing but this time in English. This is the result of attaching the label, "Severe Acute Respiratory Syndrome" (page 123) and that is the result when the label was replaced with "Love & Thanks" (page 125). They resulted in the sort of crystals both in Japanese and English. From this experiment I came to have confidence in my new idea, which is as follows:

① Water catches precisely the vibrations of words and expresses it back in crystals.
② As long as both Japanese and English words are used correctly, the reaction of the water stays the same.
③ It is better to have the information in the words as detailed as possible.
④ The words "Love and Thanks" have a very positive energy.
⑤ Even if damaged, water can regain good energy back again under a good environment (it is revivable).

Man is made mostly of water.

Therefore we too have the physical characteristics described above.

By accepting this, we can know that there is still hope left in life.

英語「Love & Thanks」の文字に貼りかえて水に見せる
Showing the replaced English words "Love & Thanks"

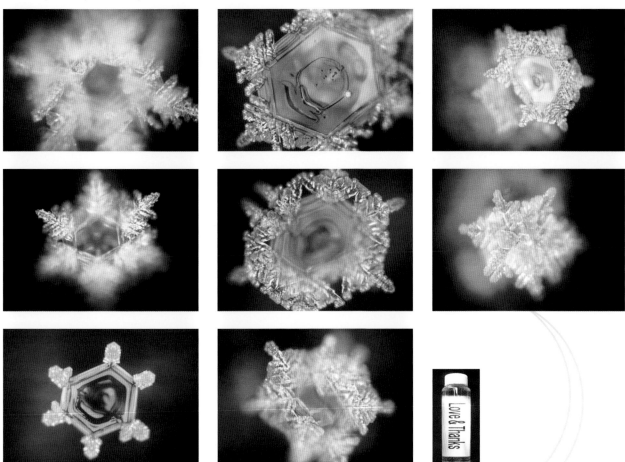

「Severe Acute Respiratory Syndrome」を見せた水に「Love & Thanks」と貼りかえ、一昼夜水に見せた後の結晶群

A series of crystals that were gained after showing the water that had seen "Severe Acute Respiratory Syndrome" the new label of "Love & Thanks" for a whole day and night.

祈りのかたちで、結晶の形は違うのだろうか？

Energy Differs Depending on the "Shape of Prayer"

　第1章でご紹介した「祈りのかたち」、それは手を合わせる合掌の形でした。そして、この形は人類にとって普遍的な「祈りのかたち」であることに気づきました。もちろんそれは手の掌を合わせる形、手の指を組み合わせる形、大きく頭上に上げ、それをそのまま地に下ろす形など、風土や宗教によって若干は違いますが、基本の形は同じだと思います。

　そこで、従来のような手をつないで輪をつくりながら祈る方法と、手をつながず、各自が手を合わせて祈る方法と、どのようにその結果得られる結晶の形が違ってくるかを実験しました。

　右の写真が手をつないだ結果、次の頁が手を合わせて祈った結果です。同じ場所、同じ人、対象の水はいつもの蒸留水、そして同じ撮影者という条件で行ったものです。

The "shape of prayer" that we introduced in Chapter 1 was that of praying hands. We noticed that this form is a universal "shape of prayer" for mankind. The style itself varies slightly from joining two palms together or lacing the fingers together to putting the hands up above the head and bringing them down to the ground. These vary depending on the climate and religion, but essentially the shape is the same.

Therefore, we carried out an experiment to see the difference in the shape of crystals obtained when we prayed holding hands in a circle and when we prayed clasping our own hands, without holding the hands of others.

The picture on the right was the result of hands held together as a group and the picture of next page is the result from individual hands in the "palms together" prayer position. The experiment was conducted under stable conditions in the same location, with the same subjects, the same distilled water and the same photographer.

手をつないで祈る
Pray by holding the hands of one another

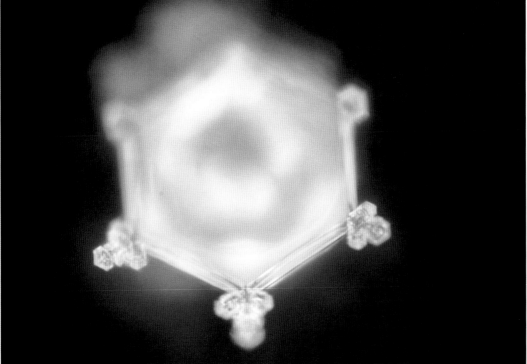

手をつないで祈った後
After praying by holding the hands of one another

祈りのかたちで、結晶の形は違うのだろうか？

Energy Differs Depending on the "Shape of Prayer"

　ごらんのように明らかに、手を合わせて祈ったほうが鮮明で美しい結晶を得ることができたのです（右頁）。すなわち、手を合わせた祈りの方がエネルギー的に高いと判断せざるを得ない結果となりました。

　この結果を得て、わたしはこの実験に参加してくれた人たちに、そのときの感じを聞いてみました。すると、みな一様に「手を合わせたときの方が雑念が起こらず、集中して祈ることができた」というのです。この実験にはわたしも参加していましたが、まったく同じように感じました。

　結局のところ、これは祈りの純粋性ということにつながってゆくのだろうと思います。このことについては後に述べますが、わたしはこれ以後、毎日のようにことあるごとに手を合わせて祈るようにし、周囲の人にもそれを勧めるようにしています。

As you can see in the picture on the right page, we could clearly obtain more clear-cut and beautiful crystals when prayer was given with the hands individually in the palm together (prayer) position. This shows clearly that the way of prayer with the hands in the "prayer position" is high in positive energy.

Having achieved this result, I asked the participants in this experiment how they felt.

They all said, "With my palms together, I could put all other thoughts out of my mind and concentrate on praying".

In truth, I also participated in this experiment, and felt exactly the same way.

All in all, I think this leads us to the purity of prayer, which will be discussed later. Ever since this experiment, I have been praying every day with my palms together, and encouraging the people around me to do so as well.

手を合わせて祈る
Pray by putting palms together

手を合わせてで祈った後
After praying by putting palms together

幸せ　Happiness

ほんとうの幸せとは何でしょうか？
自分だけが幸せってありえるのでしょうか？　自分の家族だけが幸せってありえるのでしょうか？
自分の国だけが幸せってありえるのでしょうか？　自分の住む星だけが幸せってありえるのでしょうか？

いえいえ、そうではありません。
だって、「しあわせ」はきっと四安和瀬という意味だと思うから。
四安和瀬、すなわち四方が安らぎ、和んでいる水の瀬。
「しあわせ」な水に囲まれていると、木々や草花も生き生きと緑の衣装をまとい、
おいしい空気をいつもわたしたちのためにつくってくれる。
そして、その枯れ木や葉っぱや花びらは、肥沃な土地のプロデューサー。
すべての生き物が調和する世界がうまれます。

だからみんなが「しあわせ」で、はじめてほんとうの幸せだと、わたしは思う。
でも、その幸せはどうしたら得られるのでしょう？

この宇宙を構成しているといわれる数字に聞いてみてはどうでしょう。
そう、宇宙の始まりは「1」。
そして「1」は、ぼく自身、あなた自身。

まず自分自身が幸せになりましょう。　それには？
「自分を愛すること」です。

What is true happiness?
Is it possible for only you to be happy?　　Is it possible for only your family to be happy?
Is it possible for only your country to be happy?　　Is it possible for only your planet to be happy?

No, no, it is not.
Because I like to believe that "happiness", which in Japanese is said "shiawase (幸せ)", means the same as the phrase "shi-a-wa-se (四安和瀬)".
This four-character phrase describes water that is calm and at peace in all four directions.
If they are surrounded with "happy" water, trees and flowers will be full of life, clothe themselves in green and give forth fresh clean air for us to breathe.
And their withered trees, leaves and petals are the creators in turn of rich loams.
A world is created that allows all living things to exist in harmony.

So only when all are "happy", surrounded by calm and peaceful water, can we know real happiness, I believe.
But then how can this happiness be achieved?

How about asking that number which is said to be the composer of this universe?
Indeed, the cosmos begins with "1".
And "1" is myself and yourself.

Let us each be happy first.　To do that?
"Love thyself".

おわりに

　人類は今、大きな曲がり角にきているとわたしは思います。2001年9月11日の同時多発テロによってはじまった自爆テロを中心とするテロの嵐は、その後、いっこうに収まる気配をみせていません。それどころか、ますますその地域や犠牲者を拡大しています。平和であった日本ですら、その嵐に巻き込まれてしまいました。

　アメリカは自由の擁護者の旗印の下に、懸命に世界の安寧を図ろうとしていますが、そのためにとった手法は、反米勢力を完全に目覚めさせ、蜂起させた感があります。このままではどちらかがダウンしノックアウトされるまで戦いは続きそうです。

　なんとしてもそうさせてはなりません。

　これ以上このような恐怖をつくりだす戦いが続くと、もうこの地球の体力が持ちません。そのネガティブな恐怖の波動は、この地球の血液であるすべての水の結晶を、ぐちゃぐちゃにしてしまうでしょう。

　この写真集で述べてきたこと、検証してきたことのすべては、逆もまた真なりなのです。

　そして、そうなった時、地球全体に恐ろしい疫病が発生する場ができてしまうでしょう。それがひとたび起これば、14世紀の黒死病（ペスト）どころではない、大変な数の犠牲者がでることになってしまいます。

　なぜなら、世界の人口は西暦0年のとき1.8億でした。1900年で15億、そして1950年では25億、現在は63億です。

　すなわち、ここ半世紀で38億人も増えたのです。これは異常です。あまりにも急激に増えすぎてしまって、エネルギーが乱開発、そして乱用され、それらのエネルギーは火を生みました。その結果、この地球の体温は上がり、微熱をもった人間のようになってしまいました。すなわち、人類の母体であるこの地球の免疫力が下がりに下がって、もうこれ以上下がってしまったならば……というところまできていると思うのです。

　このような状況になったのは誰のせいか？　誰のせいでもありません。わたしたちのせいです。わたしたちが何もせず、ただ不平不満ばかり言ってきたせいです。その裏には自分たち自身に対しての無力感があります。どうせ立ち上がってもつぶされるだけさ、という無力感です。

　でも、そうではないのです。この写真集で示してきたように、純粋な平和を求めての祈りは、33年前のアポロの奇跡を、今度はわたしたち人類全体にもたらしうるのです。

　みんなで祈りましょう。平和を求めて手を合わせて祈りましょう。1日に30秒でもいいから、手を合わせて祈りましょう。水からの伝言です。

In Conclusion

I think humanity is currently at an immense crossroads. The wave of terrorism, in particular the tragic suicide attacks of September 11, 2001, is far from losing its energy; rather it is expanding in both area and number of victims. Even Japan, which has been proud of its domestic peace and order, has felt compelled to get involved in this struggle.

The United Sates is fighting hard under the flag of freedom for world peace. However, the approach they took may have completely awoken anti-American forces and given rise to rebellion. If nothing were to be done, the fight would last until one side gets knocked down for the count. We cannot allow this to happen, whatever the cost. If such a war continues and creates catastrophic threats like this, the Earth will not be able to sustain its strength. Such negative waves of menace will completely destroy the crystals of all water, the blood and life stream of this planet. Conversely, what I have described and proved in this photo album is also true.

Moreover, if this happens, it will become a globally-threatening epidemic. The result will be nothing like the Black Death of the 14th century. The number of victims will be truly overwhelming. The scale of this effect must be considered proportionately.

This is because the world population was less than 180 million before the first century, 1.5 billion in 1900, 2.5 billion in 1950 and 6.3 billion at present.

This means that there has been a 3.8 billion increase during the last 50 years. This is absurdly abnormal. The population increased far too quickly and therefore much energy has been depleted and abused. The result of energy depletion was more heat. As a result the temperature of the Earth rose and the Earth has become ill, much in the same way a person can become ill. This means that the immune system of the Earth, the mother body of humanity, has been depleted down to a limit barely sustainable.

Who caused this situation? It is no single person's fault. Rather, it is our collective fault. It is because we did not do anything but complain. There is a feeling of helplessness; that getting up in the morning can bring nothing but defeat.

But no! That is not true! As I have shown you in this photo album, just as all humanity witnessed the miracle of Apollo 13 thirty-three years ago, the pure prayer for peace will bring this period to a happy ending.

Let us pray together. Let us put our hands together in prayer for peace. Only thirty seconds a day is all it takes. Let us put our hands together and pray when we wake up in the morning and when we go to bed at night. This is the message from water.

自分を愛するということ

解説

水からの伝言 自分を愛するということ

『水からの伝言 自分を愛するということ』をごらんいただいて、いかが感じられたでしょうか？

写真集ということで、できるだけご自分で思い、感じていただいたほうが良いと思い、1枚ずつに長い説明はつけませんでしたが、実は著者として、また結晶撮影技術の開発者として、お伝えしたいこと、説明しておきたいことがたくさんあります。

そう、この本では特に「祈り」というテーマについて水に問い、その答えから得たことをわたしなりに解釈して、みなさんにお伝えすることを目的としています。そのために今1歩踏み込んだ解説をこの巻末に用意させていただきました。

祈りの大切さ、その形の問題、言葉の重要性をもう1度みなさんと考えていきたいと思うのです。そして、わたしの解説をご理解いただいた方々には、「ご一緒に世界の平和を願っての『ある祈り』を実践してゆこうではありませんか」というご提案を最後にさせていただきます。その「ある祈り」とは？　結果的に、この本のタイトルである「自分を愛するということ」なのですが、それが世界の平和と結びつくのか、わたしの考えをご紹介させていただきたいと思います。

しかし、その前にまず、水を凍らせて結晶を撮影するという特異な方法がどのようにして生まれたのか？　それは今まで目に見えなかった波動というものを、目に見える形にしたものなのですが、波動とは何なのか、そして、その特徴についてお話したいと思います。

Ⅰ. 結晶写真技術を思いついたわけ

わたしはセミナーをした後の質疑応答が好きです。この中から新たに啓発されることがとても多いからです。いろいろな質問があって、それにどのように答えられるかを楽しむ自分がそこにいます。そして、それは、どちらかというと瞬間的に閃く答えが多く、わたし自身も疑問に思ってきた答えであることがしばしばです。ですから質疑応答の場は、わたしを育ててくれる場でもあります。しかし、どこの会場でも必ず質問されるのは「どうして結晶写真を撮るようになったのか」についてです。

ですから、まず、その経緯をお話ししておきましょう。

水の博士との出会い

1986年11月、わたしは縁あって、当時アメリカで開発された最新式の低周波治療器の日本総発売元の権利を得て独立し、株式会社 I.H.M.（International Health Medical）という会社を設立しました。43歳のときです。

米国製品ですから当然、アメリカ、カリフォルニアにしばしば行くようになりました。そのときのアメリカ側の代理人が、後にマイクロクラスター水を開発したリー・H・ロレンツェン博士でした。

彼は病弱だった妻のためにさまざまな療法を模索していましたが、最後にたどり着いたのが「水」だったのです。

他にも要因がありましたが、彼の人間性に共鳴したわたしは、引きつけられるように「水」の仕事に入っていきました。しかし、もとより科学者でもなんでもないわたしができたことは、彼の研究を支援することでしかありませんでした。

MRA（波動測定器）を見つける

しかし、水の領域に入っていけばいくほど、この大事な物質の実態が、実はまだほとんど何もわかっていないことに気がつきました。どうしてだろうと思い、さらに調べてゆくうちに、水の内容成分を測定する分析器はあるものの、その善し悪しを測定する機器がないことに気がついたのです。さっそくリー博士にそれを伝え、そのような測定器があるかどうか探してくれるよう依頼しました。その結果、得られたのが Bio Cellar Analyzer（生体細胞測定器）という小さな測定器でした。

同じカリフォルニアに住むロナルド・J・ウェインストックという若い研究者がホメオパシーのレメディ※用に開発したもので、もとより、水の善し悪しを測定するために開発されたものではありませんでした。

しかし、わたしはそれを一目見るなり感じるものがあって、すぐに 3 台ほど購入し、日本に持ち帰りました。そして、その測定器の名前を MRA（Magnetic Resonance Analyzer）と名付けたのです。当時まだ医療機関では血管などをスキャンする現在の MRA（Magnetic Resonance Angiography ＝磁気共鳴血管造影）は使われておらず、それを知らなかったため、開発者からその機器のコンセプトがmagnetic resonance（磁気共鳴）であると知らされて付けた名前でした。

※ホメオパシー　　19 世紀前半にドイツ人医師サミュエル・ハーネマンにより確立された療法で「同毒療法」と呼ばれる。「毒を持って毒を制す」とし、病気の症状と同じような症状を引き起こす物質を極々微量だけ体内に入れることで、逆に病気を治そうという治療法。

わたしにとって MRA は楽器だった

ところが、持ち帰ったその測定器は、操作が一般の人にはたいへんにむずかしく、すぐに倉庫で埃（ほこり）をかぶるようになってしまいました。わたしは当時、低周波治療器販売のためのアンテナショップとして、鍼灸（しんきゅう）治療院を経営していましたので、鍼灸師を何人かスタッフとして抱えていましたが、誰もこの測定器をわたしが本来意図した目的に沿うように使えなかったのです。

そのうちに良く売れていたその低周波治療器の販売の権利を、ある事情によって失い、アンテナショップも閉めざるを得なくなり、会社には売るべき商品が何もなくなってしまいました。そう、残されたのは倉庫で埃をかぶっていた MRA 3 台だけになったのです。

ほとんど絶望的な気持ちで、わたしはそれを倉庫から引っ張り出して、開発者から渡された簡単なオペレーションマニュアルをたよりに、その操作にトライしてみました。まったくの機械音痴のわたしですから、普通ならものの 30 分もしたら放り出していたであろうに、なんと 1 時間たっても 2 時間たっても、夢中でその操作に興じていたのです。

わたしは子どものころから機械や工作は大の苦手でしたが、楽器は別でした。誰にも教わらずに、いろいろな楽器を自己流ではありますが弾きこなしていました。ピアノ、ヴァイオリン、トランペットをはじめとして、新しい楽器を与えられたら、30 分後にはドレミファを奏でることができました。

今から思えば MRA は、わたしにとっての未知の楽器だったのです。マグネティック・レゾナンスのレゾナンスは共鳴という意味で、音を聞きわけることが基本となる技術でしたから、当然のこととといえば当然だったのですが、当時はその意味すら本当のところはわかっていませんでした。

MRA で波動水をつくる

以後、わたしはまるで第3の目を得たように、いろいろなもののいわゆる波動性※（それが波動だと後にわかったのですが）を測定しました。そして、念願の水を測定する技術を身につけたのです。さらに MRA には身体の中の振動の乱れを測定する機能、それを修正する振動（以後「波動」という）転写機能を備えていましたので、わたしは波動を転写するための媒体として、おりしもリー博士が完成させた特殊な水、マイクロクラスター水を選び「波動水」をつくりはじめたのです。

もともと MRA が開発された目的は、ホメオパシー治療のためでしたから、開発者はその被転写物質として 25％のアルコール溶液を使っていました。しかし、当時、まだ日本ではホメオパシーが認められていませんでしたし、ましてや医師でもないわたしがアルコール溶液を人に与えるなどしたら、すぐに薬事法や医師法に違反してしまいます。そこには、リー博士の「水」しかなかったというのが偽らざる事実で、最初から水の情報伝達力を信じ、理解していたわけではなかったのです。

ただ、水よりほかに選択すべき何物もなかった、あるいは考えつかなかったことが、今思えば良かったのでしょう。水に対して「君だけが頼りだ」「君を信頼するしかない」と思ったことが、結果的に「エネルギーの純粋性」を招いたと考えられるからです。

※波動　　　　開発者は Magnetic resonance pattern（磁気共鳴パターン）といっていましたが、わたしはこれをわかりやすく感じられる言葉として、日本語の中から「波動」という日常的に使われている言葉を選び、当てはめました。ですから、物理学用語の「波動」とは異なる用法となります。

さまざまな病に効果のあった波動水

最初は社員や身内の波動測定を行い、それにより得られた歪んだ波動を矯正するための「波動水」をつくって与えているうちに、その技法が現代医学の盲点を突くような素晴らしい効果を持つことがわかってきました。そして、それは人から人へと伝わり、わたしはいつの間にか、「波動水」という水だけで病気を治す代替医療の治療家としての道を歩むことになったのです。1987 年後半のことでした。

以後約7年間、ただ無我夢中でいわゆる病気治しの仕事を続けました。そして、さまざまな難病にも挑戦して、たいへんめざましい成果を上げることができたのです。この間、それらの成果をまとめて3冊の本も出版しました。『波動時代への序幕』(サンロード出版)『波動の人間学』(ビジネス社)『波動の食品学』(高輪出版) という本でした。

それらの本を出版した当時は、波動についての理解が進み、わたしには「波動の考え方の理解なしでは新しい世紀はない」くらいの自負がありました。しかし、本の反響は求める人ぞ求めるで、一般の人からは見向きもされないほどの売れ行きでした。

なぜ、こんなに大事で、それほどむずかしいとは思えないことが、わかってもらえないのだろう、と考え続けました。その結果得た答え、それは「人は見えないものは信用しない」ということでした。

「よし、それならば何とか見えるようにしてやろう」と持ち前の反骨精神が持ち上がり、それが現在の水の氷結結晶撮影技術の開発に結びついたのです。

「波動」を目に見えるビジュアルにして表せたら

それは 1994 年の夏のことでした。わたしは時間つぶしに立ち寄った本屋で『まだ科学が解けない

疑問』（ジュリア・ライ著　晶文社）という本を見つけ買い求めました。そして、会社に戻ってその本を開くと、目次の中から次のような項目が目に飛び込んできました。「雪の結晶には２つとして同じものはない」という項目でした。「これだ!!」と思わずつぶやきました。「雪も水ではないか、ならば水を凍らせれば必ず結晶ができるはずだ」と思ったのです。

　そして、MRA で波動を転写する前の水と、転写した後の水、もし結晶を撮影することができて、「同じ水の結晶がこのように変わった」と人に見せることができたら、「人は波動の存在を認識し認めざるを得ないだろう」。そのときのわたしは、この閃きになぜか絶対の自信を持ったことを覚えています。

水の氷結結晶写真の誕生

　1994 年の秋、わたしの閃きはみごとに具現化されました。２ヵ月ほど苦労しましたが、スタッフのうちの１人がわたしの「絶対に撮れる」という強い信念に応えてくれたのです。彼は国立大学の博士課程を卒業した立派な科学者でしたが、その年の春に入社した新入社員でもあり、純粋な男でした。その後の体験からも、水を研究する人には純粋性が絶対条件のような気がしてなりません。いろいろな試行錯誤を重ねながら、彼は２ヵ月ほどの間、たいへんな苦労をしてくれました。

　9 月に入ったある日、彼は「所長、撮れました!!」（写真：右下）と満面に笑みをたたえながら、1 枚の写真を持って、わたしの部屋に飛び込んできました。それがこの写真です。わたしは「そうか、撮れたか。ありがとう」といって、彼とがっちりと握手を交わしました。
その感激は今も忘れません。

　その日から約 5 年かけて、毎日のようにいろいろな手法で、わたしたちは水の氷結結晶写真を撮り続けてきました。水に文字を見せたり、写真を見せたりする方法は、すべて波動測定のさまざまな体験から行ったもので、わたしにとってはそれほど奇抜なアイデアではなく、するべくしてした実験です。そして、それらをまとめて写真集として世界に発表したのが『水からの伝言』（波動教育社）です。

　1999 年 6 月のことでした。

最初に撮れた水の結晶写真

　はじめて結晶写真が撮られてから今日にいたるまで、足掛け 10 年間休むことなく、わたしたちの研究所では、研究員が毎日大型冷蔵庫の中で寒い思いをしながら、さまざまな水の結晶写真を撮り続けています。はじめ 1 名の研究員、1 台の冷蔵庫でスタートしたものが、今では 6 名の研究員 3 台の冷蔵庫となりました。

　したがって最初の 5 年間と比較すると、最近の 5 年間ではその撮影枚数と種類において 3 倍以上の量となり、その結果も安定したものとなっています。

　そこで次に、本書のテーマである「祈り」に関係する過去の実験結果を、写真集の部に加えて詳細に説明させていただき、みなさまのご理解を得たいと思います。

Ⅱ. 祈りや言葉は水と結晶を変化させる　4つのケーススタディー

スタディ1　500人の波動インストラクター※の祈りの実験

　最初にこの実験で成果を得たのは、もう今から8年ほど前のことでした。東京のオフィスのわたしの机の上に水道水をおいて、全国に散らばっている500人の仲間たちに、その水に対して次のようにいってほしいと声をかけたのです。1996年2月22日午後2時のことでした。

　「東京の品川の江本所長の机の上にある水がきれいになりました。ありがとうございました」

　たったそれだけのセンテンスでした。当日2時5分、それをすぐ凍らせました。3時間半後スタッフが「そんなバカな!!」といいながら冷蔵庫からでてきました。すぐに現像に回して得られたのが、この写真（右）です。仲間たちはわたしを信頼してくれていたのですね。だからその言葉が、願いが、純粋になって距離に関係なく東京に届いたのです。

　なぜこのような実験をしたのかといえば、それは「雲消しゲーム」という遊びを友人に教えてもらい、それを試みたところ、いとも簡単に雲が消えてしまうという体験をしたからでした。これはイギリスのベティー・シャインさんがはじめたゲームで、空に浮かぶ雲に対して「雲が消えました。ありがとうございました」と過去形でいうと、雲が消えてしまうというものです。わたしは人前でもそれを何回も試して成功し、ひところは「雲消しゲームおじさん」と呼ばれたほどでした。

祈りが水道水を美しい結晶に変えた

　「なぜ、言葉だけで雲が消えてしまうのだろう」ともちろん考えました。そして波動水で人の病をたくさん治してきた体験から、「言葉の振動性」が、水である雲に対して物理的に何らかの影響を与えたのだと考えました。そして遠くにある雲も、適正な大きさであるなら、いとも簡単に消せたものですから、全国に散らばっている仲間たちに、雲消しゲームの要領で、東京の水に声を掛けてもらったのです。その後の「雪も水ではないか」という発想の原点が、ここにあったのだと思います。

※波動インストラクター　　地域、国を超えて、波動の理念を人々に伝え、その意味を教える人材を育成していくことを目的として発足した。1994年3月の第1回講習会からはじまり、以後1997年11月まで36回の講習会を行い500名を超える登録者がある。現在募集は行っていない。

スタディ2　加持祈祷によるダムの水浄化実験

水は他次元への水先案内人か!?

　結晶写真（102頁）でご紹介した加持祈祷によるダムの水の浄化実験には後日談があります。

　実験が行われてから1週間後、地元のテレビが藤原ダムから若い女性の死体が上がったことを報じ、続いてその翌日、その女性を殺した犯人が捕まったという報道があったと、加藤住職の関係者が連絡してきたのです。

　藤原ダムにはわたしを含めて3人のスタッフが行ったのですが、みんなギョっとして、祈祷前の

水の結晶写真をもう１度見直しました。そうすると明らかにその写真は女性がもだえ苦しんでいるような、そう、幽霊の写真のように見えたのです（102頁左下）。まさかと思いましたが、住職の加持祈によってその女性の魂は成仏し、時間を経て肉体までもが浮かび上がってきた、と解釈することができるかもしれません。

おまけに、祈りの後の他の写真の中から、明らかに６角形ではなく７角形の結晶の写真（102頁右下）も撮れたのですが、その意味もわかったような気がしました。６角形を３次元の世界とすれば７角形は3.5次元、すなわち霊の世界の情報ではないかと思われるのです。

わたしは「水は次元を超越して異次元の情報まで与えてくれる」のではないかと思っているのですが、それはこのときの体験による考察からなのです。

祈りこそが世界を作る設計図

さらに、このときの体験はわたしにたいへん重要なことを、その約５年後に気づかせてくれることになったのです。

それは藤原湖から持って帰った水のことです。祈祷前はもちろん、祈祷後の水もダムの水ですからかなり汚れており、ペットボトルの外からでも透明感がなく、ゴミなどがかなり混じっているのが確認されていました。その水からどうしてあのように、この世のものとも思えない結晶が撮れたのだろう、という疑問をずっと持ち続けていました（103頁）。

その疑問がようやくある事件をきっかけに解けたのです。その事件とは、あるスイスの女性が、あの藤原ダムの祈祷後の写真は自分が撮ったものだと、とんでもない主張をし、セミナーや彼女が関係する機関誌に発表したことです。2003年４月でした。

その事件は、わたしが現地の弁護士を雇って、直談判のために乗り込むという騒ぎにまで発展したのですが、結果として、それは彼女の妄想であったと本人が認め、謝罪したことで一件落着となりました。

このときに再び、何であの汚い水からあのように素晴らしい結晶が撮れ、またどうして自分が撮ったなどと、とんでもないことを言いだす人が現れたのかを真剣に考えることになったのです。それは、その女性がたんなる人騒がせな人ではない、インテリジェンスを備えた人だったからです。

その当時、わたしは「人はなぜ病気になるか」ということを「振動論」から説き、セミナーでは素粒子レベル、原子レベルでの振動の違いを説明していました。ですから、その謎を再び真剣に考えたとき、頭の中でパチンとはじけるような感じがして、次のような図が浮かび上がり、このことの解決の糸口をつかんだのです。

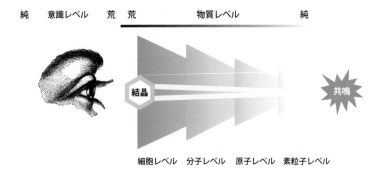

前頁の図は意識と物質レベルを描いたものですが、ゴミなどの汚れはどんなに小さくても原子レベルまでのことです。素粒子レベルには、もはやどんなに小さなものでも、それが物質性を持っている限り入ることはできません。そこは、もう完全に「波動の世界」です。つまり「意識の世界」「イメージの世界」です。

　住職の加持祈祷はそこに届きました。そして、そこに絵を書いたのです。それは、いわば原子レベル以降の、すなわち現実の3次元世界の設計図の役割を果たしたのです。ですから、湖底に沈んでいた死体が約1週間という時間差の後に、浮かび上がってきたのでしょう。

　その水を撮影した佐藤誠哉君という研究所のスタッフは、純粋な心を持った芸術家でした。彼の純粋な「真・善・美」を求める心眼は、細胞レベル、分子レベル、原子レベルにある本来なら3次元的視界をさえぎるゴミなどの浮遊物を通り超して、住職が描いた絵をキャッチした、すなわち共鳴したのです。

　共鳴は必ず「エコー現象」をともないます。佐藤君がキャッチしたその絵は、エコー現象を起こして彼の視野の中に戻ってきます。そして、実際にそこにあるかのように細胞レベルで留まります。その瞬間を捉えて佐藤君はシャッターを押したのです。

　スイスで騒ぎを起こした女性も、ある面では佐藤君的な感性を持っていたのでしょう。1度写真集で、藤原ダムの祈祷後の結晶写真を見たその瞬間から、その写真は彼女の脳裏に焼きつきました。

　そして、いつの間にか自分が撮った写真だという錯覚に陥ったのではないかと思います。ヴァーチャル世界では今後もあるようなケースかもしれません。

　以上のような考察が正しいとすれば、水の本質に大きく1歩近づいたことになるでしょう。そして、人間もいくらでもやり直しが利くことになりますし、本質的に悪人はいないことにもなります。

　まさにこれはヴィクトル・ユーゴーの小説『レ・ミゼラブル』の中の、銀の飾台を盗み捕まったジャンバルジャンと、彼の中に善なるものを見いだし、嘘の証言をして彼を釈放させた、あの司祭との関係です。ジャンバルジャンは原子レベル、分子レベルでは汚れていたけれど、素粒子レベルではまっさらであったことを、司祭の眼力は見抜いていたわけです。

　すべてのことのはじまりである素粒子という白いキャンバスに、自由に絵を描けるのは、やはり「純粋な人の祈り」そのものであることになり、ますます祈りのたいせつさが浮かび上がってくるのです。

スタディ3　　琵琶湖での祈りの実験

祈り後に琵琶湖の悪臭が消えた

　次に特筆すべき大きな体験をしたのは、1999年7月25日、言霊による琵琶湖浄化実験でした。

　当日は350人の仲間が集まってくれました。しかも朝の4時半、夜明け前です。前述したようにこの日を選んだのは古代マヤのカレンダーに則ってのことで、夜明けとともにみなで祈るとされていたからです。

　この朝、わたしたちが発したのは次の言葉でした。

「宇宙の無限の力が凝り凝って　真の大和のみ世が生り成った」

当時 97 歳になられた、医学博士でありタオイストである塩谷信男先生（しおやのぶお）が開発された大断言です。

ご高齢にもかかわらず駆けつけてくれた塩谷先生の音頭で、わたしたちは 10 回この大断言を繰り返しました。

この言葉、願いは、間違いなく宇宙に届いたのです。まずは、京都新聞同年 8 月 27 日の記事をごらんください。この記事を要約すると次のように書いてありました。

今年の琵琶湖には不思議な現象が起きている。例年この時期になるとダイオキシンの汚染度が進み、外来産の藻が異常発生し、国内産の藻がどんどん死んでいくため、悪臭が漂い、近在の住民から少なくとも毎年 300 件以上の苦情電話が関係各所に殺到していた。しかし、今年は悪臭がまったく発生せず、したがって苦情電話もない。とても良い現象なのだが、原因がわからないため当局関係者は首をひねっている。

京都新聞　1999 年 8 月 27 日付の記事

この記事を見て、わたしは興奮しました。まさかこれほどの成果がでるとは思っていなかったからです。さっそく塩谷先生に報告したところ、先生は平然として次のようにいわれました。

「当然の結果じゃ。宇宙には無限の宇宙エネルギーというものがあって、そこに届くように、みなで大断言をいった。そうしたら琵琶湖のあたりに、あのとき真の大和の場ができた。だから藻たちも仲良く共存したんじゃよ」

超音波効果によるものだった !?

しかし、正直いってそのときはまだ、わかったような、わからないような感じでしたが、その約 8 ヵ月後、わたしは別の新聞のダイオキシン関連の記事を読んで、わたしなりにすべてを理解したのです。記事の要旨は次の通りでした。

大阪府立大学の前田教授の研究チームは、このほど 20 万 Hz（ヘルツ）の超音波を水に流して、湖沼のダイオキシンや PCB を 95% 以上排除し浄化することに成功した。同研究チームの話しによると、水に超音波を発すると無数の気泡ができ、PCB やダイオキシンは本来水との親和性がないため、その気泡に入り込む習性がある。しかし気泡はその刺激によりすぐに爆発し、そのときの熱量が 5000℃にも達するので、PCB やダイオキシンが分解されて 1 つ 1 つの元素に戻り毒性がなくなる、と説明している。

産経新聞　2000 年 4 月 16 日付け　記事

わたしの理解とは次のようなものです。

わたしたちが発した声は、おそらく 300Hz 程度の振動であったろうと思います。しかし、それは非常に純粋でした。なぜなら参加した全員が塩谷信男先生を敬愛していたからです。しかも明け方の 4 時半です。環境的にも干渉波動はなく、その振動は言霊（ことだま）に導かれて宇宙のエネルギー帯に向けて

まっしぐらに飛んでいったのでしょう。そして、600Hz、1,200Hz、2,400Hz、4,800Hz、9,600Hz、19,200Hz、38,400Hz、76,800Hz、153,600Hz のそれぞれの波長帯とオクターブの理論により、「共鳴」と「エコー現象」を繰り返しながら、最終的にダイオキシンや PCB を分解してしまう周波数帯と共鳴して、それを目の前の琵琶湖の水に呼び込み、大阪府大の実験と同じ現象を招いたのではないか、と考えたのです。

　以上の考察は言霊という、どちらかといえば宗教的な現象を、「振動の原則」という科学的な尺度によってはじめて解説したものとして、将来的に認められるのではないかとわたしは自負しています。

スタディ4　　ガレリア湖から東京の水道水への祈りの実験

言葉と祈りは距離を超越する

　最後に昨年の 7 月 25 日、わたしがイスラエルのガレリア湖に行ったときの体験をご紹介することにします。

　イスラエルへは、「水への愛と感謝プロジェクト」の統一目的地として、イスラエルのヨルダン川を選び、そのためのイベントを現地の人たちの協力を得て行うために行ったわけです。

　その中で、ぜひわたしがしたかったのは、イスラエルから日本まで「祈りの言葉」を送り、それをキャッチした水を凍らせて結晶撮影をし、その変化を参加者とともに確認するという実験でした。イスラエルから日本まで、いったい何キロあるでしょうか。

　わたしは日本で、あらかじめ研究所の責任者の木津君と打ち合わせをしてゆきました。イスラエルでみなさんに「祈りの言葉」を送ってもらう時間、その言葉の送り先をイメージしてもらうためのスライドの準備、「祈りの言葉」を送った後の連絡方法、木津君が「祈りの言葉」を受けた水を凍らせて撮影するまでの時間の計算、撮影が終わって得られた画像を、イスラエルにいるわたしに送る方法などをです。

　さて、当日レクチャーに来てくれた方に、どのように説明し話したかを実況中継風にご紹介しましょう。

イスラエル・セミナー実況中継

　当日のわたしのレクチャーは現地時間の夜 11 時からの予定でした。その時間の中で、わたしは日本からの写真を受信して、会場のみなさんにお見せしたいと思っていましたので、その 3 時間半前に、時間をいただいて約 200 名ほどの来場者の前で話をはじめました。日本時間で深夜 11 時半でした。

　みなさん、今日はよくお越しくださいましてありがとうございました。わたしのセミナーは 3 時間半後ですが、その前にみなさんに協力していただきたいことがあります。これから日本の東京の、わたしのオフィスに置いてある、東京の水道水に対して「祈りの言葉」を送っていただきたいのです。

　まず日本がどこにあるのか、世界地図で確認してください（写真 1）。遠いですね。1 万キロ以上あるかもしれません。そして、東京はここです（写真 2）。さらにわたしのオフィスはここで、ここがエントランスです（写真 3）。さあイメージできましたね。わたしの部屋はこの中で、ほら、わたしが座っていますね（写真 4）。そして、その前においてある水、これが東京の水道水です（写真 5）。

いつもはこんな状態で結晶など全然できません。消毒のために塩素をたくさん入れられているからです。かわいそうですね（写真6）。

写真　1

写真　2

写真　3

写真　4

写真　5

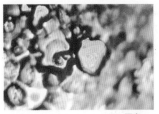
写真　6

　さあ、この水に対して「祈りの言葉」を送ってください。日本では深夜なのですが、スタッフがみなさんから「祈りの言葉」を送ってくれるのを待っています。そして、3時間後にはそれを撮影して、その写真をメールでわたしのコンピューターに送ってくるのです。それをこの場でみなさんにお見せします。ですから心を込めて送ってくださいね。それでは後に続けていってください。

Water, we love you.　　　　　　（お水さん　ありがとう）
Water, we thank you.　　　　　　（お水さん　愛しています）
Water, we respect you.　　　　　（お水さん　尊敬しています）
（これを3回繰り返した後、1分間の瞑想）
はい、ご協力ありがとうございました。また11時にお会いしましょう。

実験は成功した!!

　わたしはすぐにホテルの自分の部屋に行き、木津君に国際電話をしました。電話の向こうで、「はい了解!!」といつものように元気な声で返事をしてくれました。
　11時にセミナーがはじまりました。予定では11時半から12時ぐらいの間にメールで写真が送られてくるはずです。わたしは平静を装って、いつものように話をはじめました。しかし、内心気が気ではありません。時間はあっという間に過ぎてゆきます。もし結晶ができていなかったらどうしよう、と思いながらコンピューターの方をちらちらと見ます。やがてコンピューターに反応がありました。わたしはおもむろに会場の方たちに告げました。
　「たった今、先ほどの結果がメールで届いたようです。さてこれからメールをあけてみましょう」
当然、わたしもはじめて見るのですから、胸がどきどきです。

「さあ、どうぞ」

といって合図しました。あらかじめスライドプロジェクターにつなげてあったので、それはすぐにスクリーンいっぱいに映し出されました。会場から「ほーっ」というどよめきが走りました。そして、盛大な拍手が巻き起こったのです。わたしは一瞬目頭が熱くなり、「そうだ、これは間違いないことなんだ」とひとり深く頷いていました。その写真が109ページにもある右の写真です。

ガラリヤから東京の水に祈りが届いた

これも、先ほどご紹介した、500人の波動インストラクターの実験に成功していなければ、このような規模における実験を、試みていなかったことでしょう。そして、この実験の成功は、さらなる飛躍的な「祈りの言葉」のムーブメントにわたしを駆り立てることになったのです。

Ⅲ．波動とは何か

このように、わたしは波動測定器を得て波動水をつくり、多くの病気を治してきた実績の元に、結晶写真技術の開発に成功し、そして、いろいろな水の結晶を撮影し、観察してきました。その結果、「結晶そのものは明らかに情報であり、その情報は振動である」と確信するようになりました。それらの体験から、振動というエネルギーについて、次のような考察を得るにいたったのです。

エネルギーは振動によって生みだされる

「おわりに」の章でも述べましたが、現在の人類は混乱の迷路の中に陥ってしまったように、わたしには思えます。道に迷った場合にはどうしたらいいでしょうか？　それは振り出し、原点に戻るべきなのは、どなたも認めるところです。では、その原点とは何でしょうか？　それはわたしたちそのものの存在であり、それを生むエネルギーです。そして、そのエネルギーとは……？

「エネルギーとは振動のこと」です。なぜなら、すべてのものは原子からできており、その原子はその核において振動しているからです。有機物の場合、振動はまた命ともいえます。たとえば、わたしたちの心臓は振動していますが、その振動が止まったとき、医師はわたしたちに死を宣告します。「命」という字の真ん中に「叩く」という字が使われているのは、そのためだとわたしは思います。

ここで重要なことは、有機物の振動は自分ひとりでは、いつまでもその振動を継続することはできず、必ず第3者の力を借りて叩き続けられなければならないということです。そして、DNAあるいは自己の意思で、自動的に継続できないエネルギーである振動を、継続してつくりだす現象が「共鳴現象」です。共鳴現象には次のような特性があります。

振動数・周波数の合ったものが共振する

ここに、音叉が3つあります。そのうち2つは440Hzの音叉で、もう1つは442Hzの音叉としましょう。440Hzの音叉を叩くと、もう1つの440Hzの音叉は完全に共鳴してビーンと鳴りますが、442Hzの方はわずかに共鳴するだけで、よく耳をそば立てないと、その振動する音は聞こえません。440Hzはハ長調のラの音で、442Hzの音叉を叩いても、わたしたちの耳には、まったく同じラの音

に聞こえますが、たった 2 Hz の違いで、もう完全には共鳴しないのです。

　このように振動というエネルギーは、完全に同じ振動数の場合にのみ純粋に共鳴しますが、少しでも違う振動数だと、その違う割合において共鳴率が低くなり、やがて共鳴しなくなります。

　この原理はラジオの周波数に用いられています。昔のラジオはつまみで放送局を選びましたが、選局がうまくいったときは、ラジオの受信機の周波数と放送局の出す周波数がぴったり合ったときです。そして、ラジオにも短波放送、中波放送があるように、その波長の長さによって届く距離が違ってきます。短い波長のときの方が遠くに届く、つまりエネルギーが強いことになります。したがって、国際的な無線通信や電話はみな短い波長で通信を行っています。

真ん中の 440Hz の音叉を叩くと、同じ周波数を持った左の音叉のみが共鳴して振動音を発する。

純粋な波長がより遠くに届く

　わたしはこの波長が短い状態になることを「純粋性が増す」というように解釈しています。波長が短いと邪魔する波動が少なくなるからです。干渉波動が入り込む隙がなくなるわけです。ですから短ければ短いほど遠くに届くことになるのでしょう。

　よく禅などで座禅を組むときに「無の境地、没我の境地」になりなさいといいますが、これはさまざまな日常的なことを考えると、どうしても思考の振動に隙間がでてしまい、結果的に短い波長になれない、すなわち遠くへとその思考が飛ばないということかもしれません。ですから、無の境地になるということは宇宙情報へのコンタクトを図る波動テクノロジーなのだと思います。

　しかし、人間が音を聞ける範囲は 15 〜 20,000Hz までという物理的限界があります。遠くの音を聞いたり、逆に伝えたりすることは、その可聴音域を超える周波数帯で行わなければならないわけですから、それを行うのには自分や相手の情報を守ってくれる通信箱のようなものが、必要になってくるのではないでしょうか。

　それをしてくれるのが水で、水の中にあるという、水分子のかたまりのクラスターなのだと思います。わたしは「水は宇宙を循環している」と信じます。ですからわたしたちは水と親和することによって、水にわたしたちの情報を託し、それが相手に届けば、共鳴のエコー現象によりその返信をもらうことができるのです。したがって環境汚染などでこの地球を取り巻く大気が汚染されてしまうと、言い換えれば水が汚染されてしまうと、わたしたちは宇宙の中の迷子となり、まったく孤立無援の存在になってしまうのでは、と恐れるのです。

　瞑想というものも、このような考え方の中で、さまざまな純粋になるためのテクノロジーとして

開発考案されてきたのでしょう。以前、インド出身の経済学者であり瞑想の達人であるラビ・バトラ氏と『宇宙意識と波動』（PHP研究所社刊）を共著で出版しました。そのときに、彼が瞑想に入る状態を目の前で見せてもらいましたが、それは、それは芸術的で見事なものでした。その場所は喧騒する大都会のホテルの１室でしたが、きっと彼そのものが生来（せいらい）の純粋性をお持ちになっている方なのだと思います。

子どもたちの実験から

　波動と純粋性を確認した実験をご紹介しましょう。子どもたちが白いご飯を２つのビンに入れ、それぞれに「ありがとう」と「ばかやろう」と書いた紙を貼って、毎日、声に出して紙の通りに、それぞれに言葉をかける実験をしました。１ヵ月後に「ありがとう」の方は黄色く発酵し、「ばかやろう」の方は黒く腐ってしまいました。『水からの伝言』にその結果を発表したところ、多くの読者から反響があり、自分もこのような実験をやってみたが成功したと、写真入で報告が寄せられたのです。その例が下の写真です。

　それらの報告はすべてといってよいほど子どもたちが行った実験でした。たまに大人の方から報告がありましたが、やってみたがうまくいかなかった。あるいは１回目はうまくいったが、２回目からはダメだったというものが多かったのです。

　そうですね、子どもたちは疑いません。ところが大人はやってだめだったらどうしようとか、うまくいったぞ、次はもっと見事にやってやろう、というように思ってしまいます。つまり純粋性にかけてしまうのです。何事も疑わずそれが、なるものとして純粋に取り組む姿勢、それが波動の世界では大事なわけです。

島根県に住む小学生の女の子から報告

　実験ではイチゴやみかんなどを容器に入れたものを用意し、それぞれに「ありがとう」「愛」「こんにちは」や「ばか」の紙を書いて貼り、その他「無視をする」などの複数のサンプルを作ってその変化を観察していました。言葉の違いによって果物は変化し（良い言葉のサンプルは腐るのが遅く、悪い言葉や無視のサンプルは腐るのが早かった）、その結果報告は見事なものでした。

　一連の実験を通じて彼女の感想が非常に感動的でしたので紹介します。

　「良い心から良い言葉が生まれ、言葉が水を変え、世界を良い方向に変えることができるなら、わたしも、わたしにできることから、わたしなりの方法で世界をきれいにしていきたい。お父さん、お母さん、弟たち、友だち、そして、わたしの出会うすべての人に、心のこもった『ありがとう・大好き』をたくさんいってあげたい」

　※この他にもたくさんの実験報告が寄せられています。

Ⅳ. 手を合わせて祈ることのすすめ

　この複雑な社会で、純粋に祈るというのはなかなかむずかしいことです。ですからわたしは、「水への愛と感謝プロジェクト」の祈りのパターンを、過去の数々の「水に対して祈る」体験の中からマニュアル化したのです。

　それが、みなで手をつないで輪を作り、その輪の中に水を置いて、次の言葉を声を合わせていってみよう、というものでした。

　お水さん　愛しています。
　お水さん　ありがとう。
　お水さん　尊敬しています。

　ところが、第1章「祈りのかたち」にあるように、「祈りのかたち」の基本は両手を合わせる合掌の形であったことに気づいて、スタッフを集めて次のような実験をしてみました。

手をつないで祈る

　従来のように、手をつないで輪をつくりその真ん中に水を置き、みなで上の言葉を3回繰り返し、1分間目を瞑って祈りました。

写真1　手をつないで祈る　　　手をつないで祈った水の結晶

手を合わせて祈る

　各自が両手を合わせて「祈りのかたち」をつくり、後は同じように祈りました。

写真2　手を合わせて祈る　　　手を合わせて祈った水の結晶

　どうでしょうか？　明らかにエネルギー的に差がでていると思われませんか？
　手をつないで祈った結果（写真1）に比べて、手を合わせて祈った結果（写真2）の方が、結晶も美しくクリアです。
　その形のキレの相違は誰が見ても明らかです。そして、手を合わせたほうには、「祈りのかたち」がはっきりとでました。同じ場所で、同じ時間に、同じ人が祈り、同じ人が撮影した結果です。
　どうしてこのような差がでるのでしょうか？　わたしは実際にこの実験に参加したスタッフに聞いてみました。すると、誰もが「手を合わせて祈ったり、言葉を発した方が、雑念が起こらなくて集中できた」と答えたのです。

149

わたしもそう感じました。なぜか手を合わせると集中できるのです。そう、別の言葉でいえば、純粋になれるのです。

わたしたち日本人は、実は昔から手を合わせることには慣れていました。食事をする前、した後、仏壇のご先祖さまに対しては、ことあるごとに手を合わせていました。子どもがいたずらをして「ごめんなさい」をいうときも、「お年玉をいっぱいもらえますように」と1人で祈るときもです。

ところが、最近では手を合わせることに、気恥かしさを感じたり、宗教っぽいといって、合わせなくなった人が多いようです（そのような人も、何か大変なことがあったときは、思わず手を合わせるものですが……。DNAにはまだ残っているようです）。これは残念なことです。

わたしはこの結果を得て、本書発刊を機にして、世界の人びとに、両手を合わせて「祈りのかたち」をつくり祈りましょう、と呼びかけることにしました。

これがまず1つ、わたしがみなさまにお伝えしたいことです。

V. 自分に対して祈ろう

そして、もう1つ世界の平和のためにわたしたちが祈る方法について申しあげたいと思います。

それは「はじめに」で書いたように、最終的には「自分に対して祈る」ということです。なぜ、わたしがそのように提案するのかについて、次に説明させていただきます。

理由　1

すべてのものは、自分ひとりで振動を継続させることはできないという大原則があります。

たとえば、独楽を回すと最初は勢い良く回っていますが、だんだんとその回転数は遅くなり、やがてへなへなと止まってしまいます。車のエンジン（発動機）をはじめ、あらゆるエンジンは、燃料もしくは電気がなければ、やはり回転を続けることができません。

同じように、あらゆる生命体は、水がなければ生きてゆくことができませんが、それは、「水は振動というエネルギーを運んでくれるトラック」のようなものなので、エネルギーの補給手段を絶たれたとき、生命体は生きていけなくなるからです。

わたしたちの身体の中の60兆ある細胞も同じで、彼らは自己の振動が弱くなるとサインをだします。それが「おなかがすいた」という感覚となって伝わり、わたしたちは食べ物を摂ることになるのです。

各細胞もそれぞれの役割によって、その振動数が違いますので、振動が弱くなってくると、同じ振動数を持つ食べ物に、外から応援にきてもらって共鳴現象を起こし、再び細胞の振動を活発化させるわけです。

ところが、悪い食べ物、つまり本来の振動数を持っていない食べ物は、かえって細胞たちの生命力を阻害することになります。わたしたちが、気の合わない人といつも一緒にいると、どうしてもストレスがたまり元気がなくなってしまうのと同じです。

世界の平和を願うとか、自分以外のもののために、その幸せを願うということは、第3者に対して「良い振動を送る」という意味ですから、まず自分自身が常に元気な振動でなければなりません。そのためには、わたしたち自身が健康で幸せでなければならないわけです。

……これがすべての基本、はじまりです。

理由　2

　自分が好きで、そういう自分の存在に対して感謝を感じ、尊敬できて、はじめて本当の意味で、第3者に対して同じ思いが持てると思えるのです。結果的に、「存在」や「現象」とは、エネルギーがなければ、そこに存在し得ないし、現象として起こり得ないことなのです。その「エネルギーとは振動」です。

　振動とは、ネガティブはネガティブ同士の振動、ポジティブはポジティブ同士の振動としか、共鳴して増幅されることはないのです。いくら良いことをいったり思ったりしていても、その本質において、自分自身に対してネガティブな思いがあるのなら、相手に対してポジティブな振動を与えることはできないのです。

理由　3

　写真集の第4章、ブラジル　カラピクイバの湖の実験（106ページ）でも証明されたように、湖から採水したわずかな量の水に対して、そこに集まった20名たらずの人が、「愛と感謝」の「祈りの振動」を送ったところ、その振動は湖全体の水に伝わったわけです。

　水に対しての純粋な「祈りの振動」は、その周辺の水に対して、あっという間に同じ振動を伝える能力を持っています。

　そう、わたしたち自身が「水」であることを忘れてはいけません。

　わたしたちが輝いて、良い振動を常に発信していれば、わたしたちの周囲の「水」である人びとにそれは伝わり、やがて波紋のように世界中に広がってゆくでしょう。

　東京湾の浜辺にも、遠く異国の漂流物がたくさんたどり着いているのを、子どものころによく見たものです。

理由　4

　人はなぜ病になるのだろうかということを、波動的見地から15年ほど研究してきましたが、その最初の原因は、明らかに素粒子レベルでの振動の乱れからはじまります。

　この地球、あるいは世界人類全体を1人の人間とするならば、わたしたち1人ひとりは素粒子なのです。わたしたちの振動が乱れれば、やがてそれは、地球全体、人類規模での疾病へと移行することでしょう。

　まさに「人間は小宇宙」なのです。

　逆に、素粒子であるわたしたちが元気で幸せなら、この地球やすべての人びとも、やがて健やかで幸せになるのです。

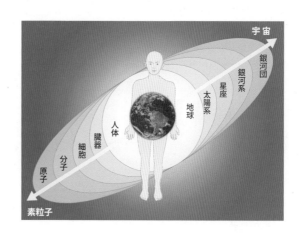

以上が、わたしが世界の平和を本当に真剣に願うならば、まず「自分自身を愛し、自分自身に感謝し、自分自身を尊敬するように願い祈りましょう」と、提案する理由です。

　自分自身が輝いて、元気な振動で他のものに元気を与える、それが本当の愛というものだとわたしは思います。

　さあ、ご理解いただけましたでしょうか？　ご理解いただけた方、良くわからなかったけれど、いい感じだと思ってくださった方、ぜひ今日から次の要領であなた自身のために祈ってみましょう。きっと何かがあなたのなかで変わってゆくことでしょう。

あなた自身のために祈る祈り

1	とき・ところ	いつでも、どこでも 朝目覚めたとき、夜寝るとき、ベッドの上で。散歩をしているとき。食事をとる前に。そのほか、ひとりで静かな時間を過ごしているときなら、いつでもどこでもいいのです。
2	思い・イメージ	自分の思いを伝えてくれる水に対して感謝の思いで世界のすべての人びとが手をつなぎ、和している情景、水の惑星地球やわたしたちの身体の水をイメージしましょう。
3	言葉	自分に対していいましょう。 ○○さん（自分の名前）　愛しています ○○さん（自分の名前）　ありがとう ○○さん（自分の名前）　尊敬しています その後に、気になっている人の名前や、波長がなかなか合わない人の名前をいってみるのも良いでしょう。
4	どのように	目を瞑り、手を合わせながらいいましょう。 いいにくければ、最初は心の中でいいましょう。そして慣れてきたら声にだしていいましょう。

　とても簡単ですね。たった３０秒の祈りです。ただし、もう少し時間をかけていただいても、もちろん結構です。

　あなた自身のために祈りはじめると、きっと何かがあなたの中で変わることでしょう。そして同じようにして、自ら変わっていく仲間が増えれば増えるほど、あなたの周囲は変わり、社会が変わり、国も変わり、世界も変わってゆくことでしょう。もちろん良い方向へと──。

The Message from Water
Love Thyself

Commentary

The Message from Water – Love Thyself

What did you feel from *The Message from Water – Love Thyself* ? Since this is a photo album, I thought it best to allow each reader to wonder and feel for themselves, so I limited the volume of commentaries. As the author and developer of the techniques of crystal photography, however, there are actually many things I would like to tell you about it.

Indeed, the purpose of this book is to ask questions of water under the theme of "prayer" and convey to you my interpretations of the answers we obtained. I prepared this section, therefore, to provide a little more detailed commentary. I would like to be able to consider with you once more the importance of prayer, the issue of its style, and the importance of words.

And at the end, for those people who have accepted my ideas, I would like to propose that we perform a "prayer" for world peace together. My proposed prayer is what the title of this book eventually became, and that is "Love Thyself". In order to explain how it is related to world peace, let me tell you my thoughts.

However, instead of getting straight into it, please allow me to explain how this unique way of freezing water and taking pictures of crystals started. The preparation of crystal pictures was to make invisible vibrations visible to us. Thus we need to know what these "vibrations" are. I would like to discuss the characteristics of vibrations.

I. The Reason behind the Technique of Crystal Photography

I like the question and answer session after each seminar, because I often find myself getting enlightened by them. Being asked various questions lets me enjoy the challenge of answering them. Many of the answers come flashing into my mind just at that moment, and very often they are answers to questions I have myself. Therefore this question and answer session gives me the opportunity to grow at the same time. The question I am always asked is how I ended up taking crystal photographs. So I will explain how it happened.

My encounter with the water expert

In November 1986 I was given the chance to obtain the sales rights to the latest model of low frequency therapy equipment developed in the United States. I became independent as a general sales agent and established I.H.M. (International Health Medical). I was 43 years old at the time.

The products were made in the USA and so I often visited California. My stateside counterpart was then Dr. Lee H. Lorenzen, who later developed micro-cluster water. He had been searching for various cures for his wife, who was in poor health, and "water" ended up being his destination after all.

There were several other reasons as well, though I resonated well with Dr. Lorenzen's personality and became attracted to his work with water. Having no background in science to begin with, all I could do was support his research.

Finding the MRA (HADO measuring equipment)

The more I associated with water, the more clearly I realized that nothing had been revealed about the actual nature of this important substance. Wondering why, I investigated further and noticed that there was analyzing equipment to measure the water's contents, but none to measure the quality of water. Right away I talked to Dr. Lorenzen and asked him to see if we could find such equipment.

What I received was a piece of small equipment called a Bio Cellular Analyzer, which had originally been developed, not for measuring the quality of water, but to develop homeopathic remedies * by a young researcher, Mr. Ronald J Weinstock, who lived in California.

But something struck me about it, so I promptly purchased three of them and brought them back to Japan. I then renamed the equipment the MRA (Magnetic Resonance Analyzer). At that time the MRA (Magnetic Resonance Angiography) that is, for example, presently used to scan blood vessels, had not yet been used and was unknown to me, and I was told from the developer that the concept of that piece of equipment was magnetic resonance.

* Homeopathy
A method of treatment based on the idea that "Like cures like" established in the early nineteenth century by the German doctor Samuel Hahnemann . It is based on the "One nail drives another" approach to cure by taking in a very small quantity of the substance that trigger the same symptom as the symptom of sickness.

The MRA was like a musical instrument to me

The equipment I brought back, however, was very difficult to operate for untrained people and soon it went to the storeroom to collect dust. I was at that time managing an institution of acupuncture and moxibustion as an "antenna" shop for the sale of low frequency therapy equipment where I had several staff acupuncturists/moxa-cauterizers. However none of them were able to use the equipment for the purpose I intended.

However after a while, due to unforeseen circumstances, I lost the right to sell the low frequency therapy equipment, even though it was selling well, and was forced to close the shop. There was nothing left to sell in the company, except those three MRAs in the storeroom covered with dust.

Almost in despair, I dragged out the equipment from the storeroom and tried to operate it following the simple operation manual provided by the developer. Being mechanically inept, I would normally give up in thirty minutes, but this time I found myself absorbed by it after a whole hour and then even two hours had passed.

I have always been terrible with machines and delicate manual work, but it was different with musical instruments. Without being taught by anyone, I had a special talent that allowed me to play, albeit in my own way, various musical instruments, including the piano, the violin, and the trumpet. Once given a new instrument, I could play a scale after about half an hour.

When I think back now, the MRA was like an unknown musical instrument for me. The key part of "magnetic resonance" being "resonance", the skill I needed was basically to distinguish different sounds, but I did not know that this meant anything at that time.

Making HADO water with the MRA

Since then it was as if I had gained an inner eye, allowing me to measure the vibration of many things. In this way I learned what I wanted so badly; how to measure water. In addition, the MRA had a function that measured the unbalance of vibrations within the body and a function to copy the vibrations (hereafter called "HADO*") in order to adjust it. I then chose the micro-cluster water that had been accomplished by Dr. Lorenzen as my medium.

The MRA had originally been developed, as stated earlier, for the purpose of homeopathy where the developer used twenty-five percent of alcohol solution as material to copy to. Homeopathy was not permitted in Japan at that time and it would have violated the Pharmaceutical Affairs Law and the Medical Act if an unlicenced person like me had given alcohol solution to people. Incidentally, there never was any doubt that there was no choice except the water of Dr. Lorenzen. It was not that I believed in or understood the ability of water to conduct information from the beginning.

I now think it was just luck then that there was no other choice than the water, or I could not think of anything else. I think after all that my feelings toward water as "you are my only hope", "I have only you to rely on" had invited the "purity of energy".

* HADO (meaning vibrations or wave motion)
Though the developer would call it a "Magnetic Resonance Pattern", I chose for it the Japanese word, "HADO" which is a common word in daily use in order to make it easy to understand. HADO here, therefore, differs in usage from the word "HADO", meaning "wave motion" in physics.

The HADO water was effective for various kinds of illness

While at the beginning I conducted the HADO measurements , and created and offered HADO water in order to correct the distortions of HADO for the company staff, families and relatives, I gradually realized that this technique implied a wonderful effectiveness to deal with a blind spot of modern medicine. Word was passed on from person to person and I went naturally along the path of alternative healer in the latter half of 1987.

After that, I worked to "cure illness" for about seven years. Having attempted various kinds of serious cases, I achieved remarkable results, which have been summarized in three published books: *Introduction to HADO Age* (Sunroad Publishing), *HADO Humanics* (Business-sha), *HADO Sitology* (Takanawa Publishing).

When I published these books, my understanding of HADO had come a long way and I had a lot of confidence in HADO, thinking things like "without an understanding of the HADO way of thinking, there will be no future". The reaction to those books were, however, that only specific kinds of people were interested in them and most people did not even pay attention to them; the books did not sell well.

I kept wondering, why do people not see how important and simple it is? The answer, I eventually realised, was that people do not believe what they cannot see. With my spirit of defiance, I was determined to make it visible, and this resulted in the development of the current technique of frozen water crystal photography.

If we could only make HADO visible···

It was the summer of 1994. I bought book entitled *The Day That Lightning Chased the House Wife: And Other Mysteries of Science* (Leigh, Julia eds., Harpercollins) that I found in a book store that I had stopped by to kill time in. I returned to my company and opened the book, then noticed the phrase "there are no two snow flakes that are alike". I heard myself murmuring "this is it!!" and I thought "snow is frozen water, and then if we freeze water, the water will be crystallized".

I thought if we were able to take pictures of water before and after the HADO is copied, and if we were able to show them to people to allow them to see how the crystals from the same water changed, people would become aware of and accept the existence of HADO. I remember feeling absolutely confident when I had this epiphany.

The birth of frozen water crystal pictures

In the autumn of 1994, my epiphany was given shape. After having suffered for about two months, one of the staff members responded to my determination that we can take pictures of crystals. He was a decent scientist and a pure man who had completed his doctorate at a national university and was a new staff member, having just entered my company in the spring of the same year. Through my experiences of this and even later, I feel that purity is an absolute requirement for the people who study water. He worked hard through a continuous process of trial and error for about two months.

One day in September he ran into my room with his face beaming and with a picture in his hand, saying "I got it, chief!" It is the picture shown on the right. Saying "Well, you got it. Thank you", we shook hands firmly with each other. I still can't forget how deeply moved I was.

After that day, for over some five years now, we have kept taking pictures of frozen water crystals through various methods almost every day. The method that shows letters and pictures to water was brought about from various experiences of HADO measurement, and the idea was nothing unconventional to me, so I adopted it naturally. Those pictures were compiled and published to the world as a photo album entitled *The Message from Water* (HADO Kyoikusha). It was June 1999.

The first crystal picture ever taken

This is the tenth year for us working with water crystal photography, where the laboratory members take pictures of all kinds of water crystals every day in the large cold refrigerators. What started with one researcher and one refrigerator has now become six researchers and three refrigerators. Thus compared with the first five years, the number and types of pictures are now three times greater and the results are more stable.

In addition to the comments made in the previous section with the presentation of the pictures, I will now introduce the results of experiments conducted in the past under the theme of this book, "prayer", to further enhance your understanding.

II. Prayers and Words Change Water and Crystals　　Four Case Studies

Study 1　　Experiment with the prayers of 500 HADO instructors*

The first success of this experiment was about eight years ago, in 1996. I put some tap water on my desk in the office in Tokyo and asked my fellow HADO instructors all over Japan to say to the water the following sentences. It was two o'clock in the afternoon on February 22, 1996:

"The water on the director's desk in Shinagawa, Tokyo has become clean. Thank you very much".

That was all they said. Then at 2:05 we froze it right away. Three and a half hours later the staff researcher came out from the refrigerator, saying "This cannot be true". The next picture is what we obtained after sending it out to develop right away (right). My fellow instructors had confidence in me, didn't they? That is why those words and wishes became pure HADO and reached Tokyo despite the distance.

The prayer has changed the tap water to form beautiful crystals

The reason why I conducted an experiment like this is that I experienced erasing clouds as easy as it when I tried "the cloud erasing game" that was taught by a friend of mine. This game was first started by Ms. Betty Shine from England; by saying to the clouds in the sky "The clouds have disappeared. Thank you very much" in the past tense (in the present perfect tense), the clouds disappear. I have erased the clouds in front of people many times and I was even called the "Cloud Erasing Game Man".

Of course I wondered why the clouds disappeared only by words. And my experience with curing many kinds of illness with the HADO water made me think that "the vibratile aspect of words" imparted some kind of physical effect to the clouds, which are made of water. Since it is possible, if the size is proper, to erase clouds in the distance easily, I asked my fellows all over Japan to send words to the water in Tokyo with the same procedure as the cloud-erasing game. My idea that "snow is also water, isn't it" came from here later on.

* HADO Instructors

The training of HADO instructors has started to create personnel who convey the philosophy of HADO and teach its meaning beyond the boundaries of regions and nations. Having started with the first training in March 1994, there have been 36 training sessions conducted as of November 1997 and more than 500 people have been registered as HADO instructors, though currently we are not recruiting anyone.

Study 2   The dam water purification experiment by incantations and prayers

Is water a pilot to the other dimensions?

There is a sequel to the dam water purification experiment by incantations and prayers introduced in this photo album (page 102). One week after the experiment, the office of the chief priest, Mr. Kato informed us that: a local TV station reported that a young woman's dead body was found in the water near Fujiwara Dam and on the following day the criminal who had killed the woman was arrested.

Three of us had gone to Fujiwara Dam and we were all shocked to hear this news. We reexamined the water crystal picture taken before the prayers. Guess what we found? It looked clearly as if a woman is writhing in pain. Yes, much like spirit photography (page 102, left below). I found it incredible, but I could also interpret it in such a way that the spirit of the woman attained enlightenment. Because of the incantations and prayers of the chief priest, the body eventually appeared.

In addition, among other pictures taken after the prayers, there were some pictures of heptagonal crystals instead of hexagonal (page 102, right below). Regarding the above fact, I felt I understood the meaning behind it. If hexagonal denotes a three-dimensional world, then septagonal denotes the 3.5 dimensional world, which made me think it must be information from the world of sprits. I have been thinking that water transcends dimensions and gives us information about other dimensions. This conclusion is based on this experience.

Prayer is a blueprint to create the world

Furthermore, after five years, this experience made me realize a very important thing.

It is about the water brought back from Lake Fujiwara. Both before and after the prayers, the typical dam water was obviously dirty. We could observe through the plastic bottle that it was not clear, and was polluted. I had been questioning how we could obtain such beautiful, unearthly crystals from such water (page 103).

That question was finally solved. The discovery was brought about by one incident; a Swiss woman made an absurd claim that she took that Fujiwara Dam picture and announced this in her seminars and associated bulletins. This was April 2003.

This irritation developed to the extent where I hired a local attorney and went to negotiate with her personally. It was finally settled and she personally admitted it was her fantasy and apologized.

Because of this incident, I again thought seriously how we could have achieved such wonderful crystals from such dirty water. I also wondered why someone would appear and make the crazy claim that she took that picture. She was clearly not a publicity-seeker, but a person with intelligence.

At this same time, I had been advocating "why people get sick" from the point of HADO theory, through illustrating the difference in vibration level between elementary particles and atoms. Subsequently, when I seriously thought about the mystery again, I felt something snap in my head and a diagram came to me that provided clues to follow in order to solve this mystery.

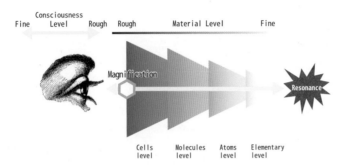

This is a diagram that describes the layers inside the human body. No matter how small pollutants and other trash are, they can only reach down to the atomic level. At the level of elementary particles, no matter how small something is, as long as it has materiality it cannot enter. It is already a complete "World of HADO", that is, "The world of senses and images".

The chief priest's incantations and prayers reached that area and created a picture there. It played the role of drawing in the actual three-dimensional world beyond the atomic level. That probably is why the dead body that was sunk to the bottom of the lake came to the surface after a time gap of approximately one week.

Mr. Masaya Sato, a staff member of the laboratory who shot the picture of the water, is an artist who has a pure heart. His pure mind's eye that seeks for "Truth · Virtue · Beauty" went through the suspended substances and pollutants that normally block the view of the three-dimensional field in the cellular, molecular, and atomic level. He captured the picture that the chief priest drew. In other words, he resonated.

Resonance always accompanies the "echo phenomenon". The picture that Mr. Sato captured gave rise to the echo phenomenon and it returned to his sight. Then it stayed at the molecular level as if it had always existed there. Mr. Sato caught that moment and released the shutter.

The woman who caused the disturbance might have, to some extent, had an ability similar to Mr. Sato's. From the moment when she first saw that crystal picture, the picture stayed in her mind. Without realizing it, she fell into the illusion that she took the picture herself. In the virtual world, this may be the sort of case that occurs again.

If the above assessment is correct, we have made a big step toward understanding the essence of water. This would mean that man can start again any number of times, and that essentially there are no bad people.

This is exactly the relationship between Jean Valjean in the novel, *Les Miserables* by Victor Hugo, who got caught for stealing a silver decorative stand and the pastor who found the goodness in Valjean and committed perjury to allow him to go free. The pastor could see, through insight, that Valjean was tainted at the atomic molecular levels, but he was clean at the level of elementary particles.

One could conclude that what can be freely drawn on the white canvas called the elementary particle level is "the prayer of a pure person itself" and this makes clearer the importance of prayer.

Study 3   Experiment of prayer Lake Biwa

The bad odor disappeared after the prayer

The next notable experience deserving special mention happened on July 25, 1999. It was the Lake Biwa purification experiment using the "Kotodama" - the power of words. Some 350 members gathered before dawn that day at 4:30 in the morning. As I mentioned before, I chose that day in accordance with the ancient Mayan calendar and the tradition that they prayed together at the crack of dawn.

What we said that morning was the following phrase:

"The infinite power of the universe coalesced, took solid form, and created a truly harmonized world".

It is a grand affirmation created by Tao Master Nobuo Shioya, who was 97 years old at that time. Under the direction of Master Shioya, who joined us eagerly in spite of his great age, we repeated the grand affirmation ten times.

These words and wishes surely reached out to the universe. The story is already very famous so I am sure many people know, but please take a look at the article from the "Kyoto Newspaper" of August 27 the same year. The summary of this article is as follows:

Kyoto Newspaper - article dated August 27, 1999

A mysterious phenomenon is occurring in Lake Biwa this year. Usually, at this time of year, we have an abrupt increase of algae of foreign origin that kills domestic algae due to the progress of the pollutant dioxin. This normally creates a foul odor and over 300 phone-call complaints from the neighboring residents pour into the relevant offices every year. This year, however, there is no odor; therefore no complaints calls were received. Although this is a very welcome phenomenon, the reason is unknown. The authorities concerned are wondering what it might be.

Kyoto Newspaper

I got excited seeing this article since I was not expecting a result as spectacular as this. I reported this news to Master Shioya and, with composure, he said as follows:

It is the obvious result. There is an infinite energy in the universe and we said the great affirmation together to reach it. Then it created a true and great harmonious field around Lake Biwa. That is why the algae coexisted in harmony.

Was it the effect of ultrasonic waves!?

To be honest, at that time I felt unsure whether or not I truly understood what had happened. About eight months later, I understood everything after reading another newspaper article about dioxin. The summary of this article is as follows:

Sankei Newspaper - article dated April 16, 2000

A research team led by Professor Maeda of Osaka Prefecture University succeeded in the purification of lake and marsh water. They eliminated more than 95 percent of the dioxin and PCB in these lakes and marshes by running ultrasonic waves of 200,000 hertz to the water. The research team explained that when ultrasound waves are sent to water, countless bubbles are formed and PCB and dioxin enter those bubbles because their nature has no affinity for water. Reacting to the stimulation, however, the bubbles soon explode. This releases heat, which reaches 5,000 ℃ , causing PCB and dioxin to break down into their component non-toxic elements.

Sankei Newspaper

My interpretation of this is as follows:

I believe the choral voice we made was, in all probability, vibrations near 300 hertz. It was in fact, very pure. This is because everyone who participated adores Master Nobuo Shioya. In addition, it was 4:30 at dawn. There were fewer interference vibrations in the environment. The vibrations would have been led by Kotodama: the power of words, and would have flown straight into the energy zone of the universe.

My theory was that based on the idea that of the octave theory (similarity theory) and each 600 hertz, 1,200 hertz, 2,400 hertz, 4,800 hertz, 9,600 hertz, 19,200 hertz, 38,400 hertz, 76,800 hertz, and 153,600 hertz wavelength zones repeated their resonance and echo phenomenon and finally resonated with the frequency zone which resolves dioxin and PCB. Then they were brought back to the water of Lake Biwa in front of us to trigger the same phenomenon as the experiment at Osaka Prefecture University.

I am confident that the above view will be accepted in the future as to comment on Kotodama; the power of words that is rather a religious phenomenon on a scientific scale, "Principles of Vibrations".

Study 4   The experiment of prayer from the Sea of Galilee to the tap water of Tokyo

Words and prayers transcend distance

Finally I would like to tell you what I experienced when I went to the Sea of Galilee in Israel on July 25, 2003.

This visit to Israel was for the "Project of Love and Thanks to Water" the purpose of which was to send love and thanks to the water of the world. I chose the River Jordan to hold an event with the support of the local people.

The experiment I was hoping to conduct was to send the "words of prayer", the power of words, from Israel to Japan and examine it with crystals. How many kilometers are there from Israel to Japan? It is probably about 10,000 kilometers.

To confirm beforehand the details of the experiment, I had a meeting with Mr. Kizu, who is in charge of the laboratory in Japan. The discussions centered around the time we would send "the words of prayer" from Israel, the words to be sent and the preparation of slides so that the people in Israel can see where they are sending their words to. We also discussed how to contact each other after sending the words of prayer, the calculation of time taken for Mr. Kizu to receive it, freeze the water and take photos, and how to send the images captured back to us in Israel.

Now I will tell you how I explained to the people who came to my lecture, like a live on-the-scene report.

Live broadcast of the seminar in Israel

My lecture on that day was scheduled for 11:00 p.m. local time. I was hoping to show everyone the pictures to be received from Japan, so three hours ahead of time I asked for some time and started to talk to the audience of about 200 people. It was 11:30 at night, Japan time.

Ladies and gentlemen, thank you for coming today. My seminar won't start for three and a half hours but, before my seminar, there is something I would like to ask your cooperation for.

I would like to ask you to send to Japan the "words of prayer". Specifically speaking, to the Tokyo tap water that is standing in my office in Tokyo. First of all, please check where Japan is on the world map (picture 1). It's a long way, isn't it? It may be more than 10,000 kilometers. And this is Tokyo (picture 2). Here is my office and this is the entrance (picture 3). Can you picture it now? My room is in here and I am sitting as you can see (picture 4). The water is standing in front of me. This is the Tokyo tap water (picture 5). Usually the water is in this condition and it forms no crystals, because the water contains a lot of chlorine for sterilization. Isn't that pathetic? (picture 6)

picture 1

picture 2

picture 3

picture 4

picture 5

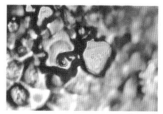
picture 6

Now, please send the "words of prayer" to this water. In Japan, it is late at night, but my staff member is waiting for you to send the "words of prayer". Then, three hours later, he will take a photo and mail it to my computer. I will show it to you here. So please send the words with your whole heart. Now, please sing in union after me.

Water, we love you.
Water, we thank you.
Water, we respect you. (having this repeated three times and with one minute of meditation)

OK, thank you for your cooperation. See you again at 11:00.

The experiment was successful!!

Right away I went to my hotel room and made an international call to Mr. Kizu. On the other end, I heard, Yes, OK! Mr. Kizu, as usual, answered in a cheerful voice.

At 11:00, my seminar began. The picture was tentatively scheduled to be received by mail between 11:30 and 12:00 o'clock. Pretending to be calm, I started to talk as usual. However, in my heart, I was beside myself with worry. Time passed before I knew it. I was worrying what to do if no crystals were found as I glanced occasionally at the computer. Then eventually there was a reaction from the computer. I then declared to the audience in the venue:

"The result of the Kotodama has apparently just now come by e-mail. Now let's open the mail and see. Of course, I will see it for the first time as well; so my heart is pounding".

The computer had been already connected to the slide projector, so the image was projected on the screen in large scale. Throughout the venue swept a stir, a murmur of "OOOOOHHHH". Then the sound of tremendous applause was drowned it out. For a moment I was moved to tears and murmured "Yes, this is absolutely true". The picture shown on page 109 is the picture.

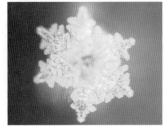

The prayer from Galilee reached the water in Tokyo

This is another example of an experiment that, if I had not had the success in the experiment with 500 HADO instructors I introduced earlier, I would not have even thought about doing on such a grand scale. The success of the experiment again drove me further toward the "words of prayer" movement.

Ⅲ. What is HADO?

Having managed to obtain the HADO measuring equipment and produce the HADO water, and having been able to cure a number of illnesses, I succeeded in the development of the technique of crystal photography and since then I have been taking and observing pictures of various water crystals. As a result, I have come to firmly believe that "crystals themselves are clearly information and that information is in the form of vibrations". After having experienced all that, I now have the view that I describe below about vibrations as energy.

Energy is created through vibrations

As I said under the section, "In Conclusion", I believe that modern society has got itself into a maze of confusion. When you get lost, what should you do? To that question, everybody would agree that we should return to the starting point. Then what is that starting point? It is our existence itself and the energy that created it. Then what is that energy?

"Energy is vibrations". Because everything is made of atoms and the atoms vibrate in their nucleus. In case of organic matters, we can say the vibrations are life. For example, our hearts are vibrating. When it stops vibrating, the doctor will declare death. That is why I think in that the middle of the character for life, 命 is found the character that means "to beat": 叩 .

The problem is that the vibrations of organic matter cannot vibrate automatically for ever. To continue vibrating, they require the help of the third party. In addition, the "resonance" is the phenomenon that creates continuous vibrations, which are energy that cannot sustain itself with DNA or by one's own will. The resonance phenomena has the following characteristics.

The matching of frequencies creates a sympathetic vibration

Take three tuning forks. Two are 440 hertz and one is 442Hz. When we sound one of the 440Hz tuning forks, the other 440Hz tuning fork resonates fully, buzzing, but the 442Hz tuning fork resonates only slightly. We must listen for the sound of vibrations attentively. 440Hz is the "La" sound in C major. When the 442Hz tuning fork is struck, it produces the same La sound to our ears, but with only 2Hz difference it does not resonate completely. As explained above, vibrations (energy) resonate only with the same frequency.

The slightest frequency deviation reduces the possibility of resonance and it eventually stops resonation.

This principle is used for radio frequencies. We used to select a radio station with a channel selection dial. We succeed in tuning when the frequency of the receiver in the radio and the frequency from the radio station match. In addition, as radio has short and medium wave broadcasting capabilities, the length of the wave determines the distance of reach. Shorter wavelengths reach further. In other words, the energy is stronger. Therefore, all international wireless communications and telephones are performed using short wave lengths.

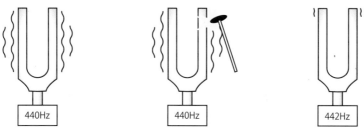

Striking the tuning fork of 440HZ in the middle, only the left tuning fork, with the same frequency, resonated and made a vibrating sound

Pure waves reach further

I interpret the situation when waves become shortened as an increase in purity, because when the wave is short, interfering vibrations decrease. There is less space for disturbing vibrations. Therefore, the shorter wave can reach further.

When sitting in Zen meditation, we are told to find a spiritual state of nothingness - a state that transcends self. This may mean that when we think about things in the normal course of our daily lives that gaps open up between the vibrations of our thoughts, preventing the creation of short waves, thus preventing our thoughts from reaching very far. I believe, therefore, that entering the state of nothingness is a "HADO" technology that allows us to come into contact with cosmic information.

Human beings, however, have physical limitations regarding the range of sounds able to be heard. It is from 15 hertz to 20,000 hertz. To hear or transmit sounds far away, it must be done in a frequency band exceeding the scope of our capability. Therefore, in order to do this, there probably should be something like a communication box that protects our or our counterpart's information.

What allows us to accomplish this is water, and the molecular clusters in it. I believe water circulates around the universe. Thus, by having an affinity with water, we can entrust our information to water. When the water reaches our counterpart, we can receive a message back from it through the echoing of resonance. Therefore, when the surrounding air of the Earth gets contaminated due to environmental pollution, the water also gets contaminated. We become a lost child in the universe and get anxious that we are becoming completely alone and living an unaided existence.

But considering this, meditation may be developed and designed as one of various technologies to allow one to become pure. I have published a book, *Awareness for the universe and HADO* (PHP institution Inc.) in collaboration with Dr. Ravi Batra, an economist and master of meditation from India. On one occasion, I had a chance to see him going into meditation. It was such wonderful art. Even though it was in a hotel room in the middle of a busy city, I felt that he was truly a man of pure character according to nature.

From the children's experiment

Let me tell you about an experiment to confirm the connection between HADO and purity. The children prepared two bottles of cooked white rice with a label attached to each bottle, one saying "Thank you" and the other saying "Idiot". And they also repeated aloud to each bottle daily what the label said. One month later the rice with "Thank you" had fermented to a yellow colour and the rice with "Idiot" had spoiled and gone black.

When presented with the results in *The Message from Water*, many readers responded; they reported, with pictures, as they did the same type of experiments and how they succeeded. One of the pictures is shown below.

Almost all of the reports made were the results of experiments conducted by children. We received a few reports from adults, but in many cases they say that they attempted it but did not go well. The results were completely opposite, or it went well the first time but didn't the second time.

That's right - children do not doubt. On the contrary, it is adults who tend to doubt, thinking such things as "What should I do if it doesn't turn out right", or "It went well; OK, next time I will do even better". That is to say, it is a lack of purity. It is important not to doubt, to have a pure attitude for approaching it and accepting it as it goes. This is important in the world of HADO.

A report from a primary school girl living in Shimane Prefecture

For the experiment she prepared containers containing strawberries, oranges and other fruit, and she made several kinds of samples; labeled variously as "Thank you", "Love", "Hello", and another other sample was labelled "Ignored". She observed how they changed. Depending on the words, the fruit changed differently; the samples with good words took longer to get spoiled and the samples with bad words and ones ignored spoiled quickly. The reported results were wonderful.

Her comments from her experience with a series of experiments were very moving, so I will share them with you:

"If good words are created by good hearts and good words change the water to make it possible to change the world for the better, I would like to start with what I can do to change the world for the better. I would like to offer many 'Thanks, I love you' calls from my heart to my father, mother, brothers, friends and all the people I meet".

※ Many other experiments have been reported in addition.

IV. A Recommendation to Put Your Hands Together and Pray

It is rather difficult to pray purely in this complicated society. That is why I wrote a manual based on my many experiences with the pattern of prayer to water derived from the "Project of Love and Thanks to Water". The manual states that we should make a circle holding hands with one another, put the water in the center of the circle and chant together the following phrases:

Water, we love you.
Water, we thank you.
Water, we respect you.

However, as stated in Chapter 1, "The Shape of Prayer", I realized that the "shape of prayer" was the form of "praying hands" and I gathered my company staff to conduct the following experiment.

① Pray by holding the hands of one another

As usual, we made a circle, held hands and put the water in the middle. We repeated the above phrases three times and prayed for one minute with our eyes closed.

② Pray by putting palms together

Each put hands together individually and formed the "shape of prayer" and prayed as above.

① Pray by holding the hands of one another

① After praying by holding the hands of one another

② Pray by putting palms together

② After praying by putting palms together

These are the results:
What do you see? Don't you think there is a clear difference in energy levels?

Compared with the result of holding hands, the crystal obtained from the praying hands is clearer and more beautiful. The difference in its clear-cut shape is obvious to anyone's eyes. In addition, the "shape of prayer" could be clearly identified with the crystal from praying hands. In the same place, at the same time, the same person performed the prayer and the same person took the photographs.

What caused this difference? I asked the staff who actually participated in this experiment. Everyone answered, "I could put other thoughts out my mind and have better concentration when I put my hands together in prayer and said the words". I felt the same. For some reasons, we can concentrate better with our hands together. In other words, we can be pure.

We Japanese, in fact, were accustomed to putting hands together in the past. We still put our hands together from time to time; before and after meals and in front of the family Buddhist altar. This is also the way in which children apologize for being mischievous and when they wish for a lot of New Year's presents.

Recently, however, there are many people who maybe feel hesitant to put their hands together, or who rarely do so because they feel it is too religious (though even such people, in spite of themselves, put their hands together when something terrible happens ⋯ maybe it has remained in their DNA). It is a pity.

Having obtained the above results, and commemorating the publication of this book, I have decided to call out to my fellow global citizens. Let us pray by putting our hands together in the prayer position.

Ⅴ. Pray to Yourself

I would like to discuss one more thing; the method of our prayer for world peace. It is after all, as I expressed in the Preface, to "pray to yourself". Let me explain why I propose this.

Reason 1

There is a principle that nothing can continue vibrating all by itself. For example, when you spin a top, at the beginning it spins vigorously, but soon it loses its force and stops spinning. All kinds of engines or motors, including car engines, cannot continue running without fuel or electricity.

In the same way, no life can live without water, because "water is like a truck to deliver the energy that is called vibrations"; when the means of energy supply is lost, no life form can live.

The 60 trillion cells of our body are the same way, and send a signal when their vibrations are becoming weak. It is expressed as the feeling of "hunger" and therefore we take food then. Each cell has a different role so has a different vibration frequency. When the vibrations become weak, it requires the support of food with the same vibration frequency to create a resonance phenomenon and activate the vibrations of the cell again.

Bad food, however, in other words, the food that does not have a required frequency level, disturbs the vitality of cells instead. It is the same as when we are with someone all the time with whom we do not get along; we get stressed and lose vitality.

Wishing for world peace, wishing on behalf of someone other than yourself means "sending good vibrations to other people", so you yourself need to be always vibrating in good health. For that reason, we ourselves need to be healthy and happy. This is the basis of everything, the beginning of it all.

Reason 2

I believe only when you like yourself, feel grateful to your existence itself, and when you can respect yourself, only then are you able to have the same feelings toward other people. After all, the "existence" and the "phenomenon" cannot exist without energy and cannot rise as a phenomenon. That is, "energy is vibrations".

The nature of vibrations is that negative resonates only with negative and positive resonates only with positive. No matter how much you say and think good things, you cannot give off positive vibrations as long as you have a negative image of your substance.

Reason 3

As proved in the experiment at a lake in Carapicuiba in Chapter 4 (page 107), when the group of less than twenty sent the "vibrations of love and thanks prayer" to the small amount of water taken from the lake, the vibrations were spread all over the lake.

The "vibrations of pure prayer" to the small amount of water are capable of conveying the same vibrations to the surrounding water.

Indeed, we should not forget that we ourselves are "water".

When we shine and keep sending out good vibrations, they reach the people and the "water" around us and eventually they spread like ripples all over the world.

When I was a child I used to see that a great deal of flotsam and jetsam from distant countries had reached the shores of Tokyo Bay.

Reason 4

I have been studying why people get sick, from the point of view of HADO, for about fifteen years. It is clear that sickness is primarily caused by the distortions of vibrations at the level of elementary particles.

If we assume the Earth or the entire global human race is a person, each one of us is then an elementary particle. The distortions of each of us will grow to become the sickness of the entire Earth or the whole human race.

Indeed, "Man is a microcosm".

On the contrary, if we as elementary particles are strong and happy, this Earth and all the people on it will become healthy and happy.

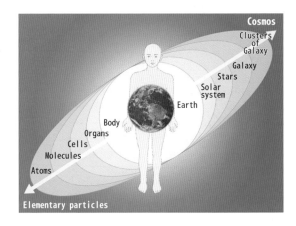

This is the reason why I propose to "wish and pray to first love yourself, be grateful to yourself, and respect yourself".

We should ourselves shine and have strong vibrations, and then give our vigorous spirit to others. I think that is true love.

Do you think you understand what my idea is? To those who would accept this idea, or those who think that this sounds good even if they don't fully understand it, let us pray for ourselves from today with the following procedure. I am sure something will change in yourself.

Prayer to pray for yourself

1	Time · Place	**Anytime, anywhere.**
		When you wake up, when you go to bed, in bed. When you are taking a walk. Before taking a meal. Anytime anywhere when you are alone spending a quiet time is OK.
2	Feelings · Image	**With feelings of thanks to the water which convey your feelings.**
		Picture all the people in the world holding hands with one another in harmony, and our water planet, the Earth, and the water of our bodies.
3	Phrases	**Let us say to ourselves:**
		(Your name) I love you
		(Your name) I thank you
		(Your name) I respect you
		After this, it is also good to say the name of a person who you are concerned about or who is on a different wavelength.
4	How	**With your eyes closed and your hands put together.**
		If it is difficult to say aloud, say it in your heart first. Then when you get used to it.

It's very easy, isn't it? Each prayer lasts only thirty seconds. Of course it's no problem if you want to take a little longer.

When you start praying for yourself, something will definitely change in yourself. And when more and more of your fellow men change in the same way, your surroundings will change, society will change, the country will change and the world will change, all in a good direction, of course ——— .

結晶撮影の現場から

IHM 総合研究所　木津孝誠

　写真集に登場する結晶映像は、以下のような手順で撮影を行っています。ここでは72〜75ページにあるスカトー寺での3つのサンプル観察の実験を例に、結晶観察の全体と、それぞれのサンプルから得られる結晶パターンの傾向性の違いについて説明します。

検体（水）を凍らせる際の手順

① 　1サンプルあたり50枚のプラスチック製のシャーレに水をスポイトで0.5ccずつ滴下します（写真1）。

② 　シャーレに蓋をしてフリーザーに収めます。

③ 　フリーザーは最低冷却温度がマイナス25℃まで下がるもので、3時間かけてサンプルを氷結させます。

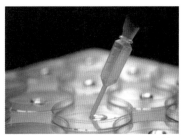

写真1

結晶撮影の手順

① 　氷結したサンプルを観察する場所は大型冷蔵室（1坪程度）で、室内はマイナス5℃に設定してあります。

② 　観察用顕微鏡は「金属光学顕微鏡（カメラ装置付き）」（写真2）です。
　　冷凍庫から1つずつシャーレに載った氷結サンプルを取り出し、顕微鏡の上にセットします。

③ 　氷結したサンプルは隆起しており（写真3）、その頂点に顕微鏡から落射される光を当てます（写真4）。

④ 　接眼レンズを覗いて結晶を観察し、顕微鏡に設置されたカメラで撮影します。

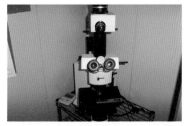

写真2

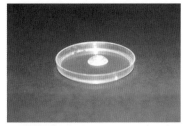

写真3

結晶写真撮影使用機材

・OLYMPUS製　システム金属光学顕微鏡　BX60

・OLYMPUS製　全自動顕微鏡写真撮影装置　PM10SP

フィルム

・FUJICOLOR　業務用カラーネガフィルム　ISO400

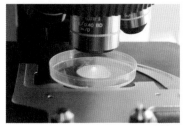

写真4

観察基準

　結晶はその形状によっていくつかのタイプ（美結晶、美傾斜、6角形、放射状、格子状、不定形、陥没、無し）に分類しています。

　結晶形状のタイプによって0点から100点までの点数をつけます。形状分類ごとにその点数と観察された氷結サンプル数の積数を算出します。その総合点数の50氷結検体平均が結晶評価点数となります。

　点数の基準となるのは、結晶形状が6角形であるかどうかに加えて、美しいかどうかであり、その判断は観察者が行います（例：6角形で美しい結晶＝100点、結晶無し＝0点）。

　この算出方法は、観察者による評価点数のばらつきはあるものの、サンプル水の結晶状態の傾向は得ることができます。

タイ スカトー寺の水の結晶

試料	美結晶	美傾斜	6角形	放射状	格子	不定形	陥没	無し	評価点数
A　村人の家の甕の雨水	1	3	1	0	3	41	1	0	28.8
B　森の中の甕の雨水	1	7	1	0	1	38	2	0	38.2
C　　　寺の甕の雨水	3	6	3	0	2	36	0	0	41.8

　3つの甕（かめ）の雨水の結晶観察全体をあらわす表、およびグラフからもわるように、美しい結晶が多ければ多いほど評価点数は高くなります。また観察された「美結晶」並びに「美傾斜」の結晶パターーンの数の違いだけを見ても、村にあった甕の雨水よりも、寺や森にあった甕の水の方が美しい結晶が観察される確率は高いといえます。よってそこから、場が持つエネルギーの違いを結晶観察によって推測することが可能といえます。

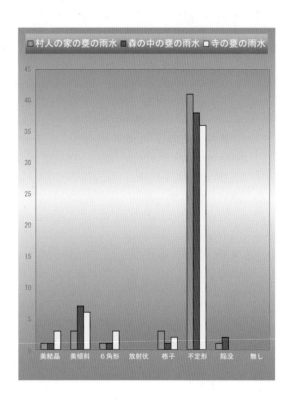

Crystal Photography in the Laboratory

Takashige Kizu
Manager
IHM Research Institute

The crystal pictures you see in this photo album are prepared using the following procedure. In this section, I will explain crystal observation in general and note the different trends of crystal patterns obtained from each sample using as an example the three sample observations in Sukato Temple seen on page 72-75.

The procedures for freezing the specimen (water)

① From each sample, 0.5cc of water is dropped using a syringe onto fifty separate plastic petri dishs (picture 1).

② The petri dishes are then covered and stored in a freezer.

③ The freezer is capable of cooling to at least $-25\ ℃$. The samples are frozen for three hours.

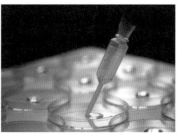

picture 1

The procedures for taking crystal pictures

① Frozen crystal samples are observed in a large refrigerated room (about 3.3 m^2) set at a temperature of $-5℃$

② The microscope used for observation is a metal light microscope with a camera (picture 2).
Each frozen sample is taken out one at a time from the freezer on the petri dish and is set on the microscope.

③ The frozen sample has a swelling in the middle (picture 3), and it is on this swelling that light is projected down from the microscope (picture 4).

④ The crystals are observed through the eyepiece and photographed by the camera mounted on the microscope.

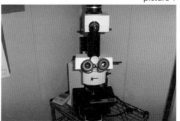

picture 2

Equipment used for the crystal photography
· OLYMPUS System Metal Light Microscope BX60
· OLYMPUS Full Automatic Photomicroscope PM10SP
  Films
· FUJICOLOR Professional-quality Negative Color Film ISO400

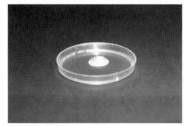

picture 3

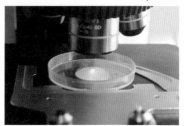

picture 4

Observation criteria

Crystals are classified in accordance with the types of their shapes (Beautiful, Semi-beautiful, Hexagonal, Radial, Lattice, Irregular, Collapsed, None)(See the top of the table).

Each type of crystal shape is allocated with a score from zero to a hundred. The Multiple of each sample observed are added up for each classification and the average score of the fifty specimens from the total points becomes the crystal evaluation score (See the right column).

The scoring criteria is based on whether the crystal is hexagonal or not, as well as whether it is beautiful or not, based on the judgment of an observer (For example, a beautiful hexagonal crystal = 100 points; no crystal = 0 points).

Though this method of calculation of the evaluation score does have discrepancy between observers, I believe it is possible to at least see the overall trend of the crystallization of the water sample.

Water Crystals of Sukato Temple

Samples	Beautiful	Semi-beautiful	Hexagonal	Radial	Lattice	Irregular	Collapsed	None	Multiple
A Village rainwater	1	3	1	0	3	41	1	0	28.8
B Forest rainwater	1	7	1	0	1	38	2	0	38.2
C Temple rainwater	3	6	3	0	2	36	0	0	41.8

As shown in the graph and the table that presents the overall observation of the rainwater crystals from the three jars, the greater the number of beautiful crystals that are observed, the higher the evaluation score. Furthermore, even the difference in the number of crystal patterns between "Beautiful" and "Semi-beautiful" shows us that the rainwater contained in the jars in the temple and the forest has a greater chance of providing beautiful crystals than the rainwater in the jar in the village. Therefore it can be concluded that crystal observation allows us to makes assumptions about the differences in energy levels existing in each place.

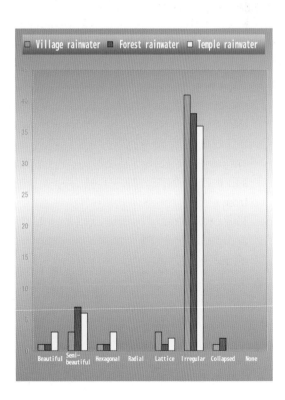

INDEX

著者　江本　勝　えもと まさる

　1943 年、横浜生まれ。横浜市立大学文理学部国際関係論学科卒。86 年、株式会社 I.H.M を設立。92 年 10 月に「オープン・インターナショナル・ユニバーシティ」より代替医療学博士の認定を受け、ライセンスを交付される。アメリカで共鳴磁場分析器やマイクロクラスター水に出合い、オリジナルな視点から水の研究に取り組み、その成果である『水からの伝言』(波動教育社) は世界 17 カ国で翻訳され、大きな反響を呼んでいる。波動技術のパイオニアとして日本に「波動」を広めた第一人者でもある。日本をはじめ世界各地で水と波動と結晶に関する講演活動を精力的に行っている。I.H.M. 総合研究所所長株式会社 I.H.M 代表取締役、国際波動友の会会長。

　著書に『水からの伝言』『水からの伝言 Vol.2』『いのちからの伝言』『水は語る』(波動教育社)、『水は答えを知っている①』『水は答えを知っている②』『結晶物語』(サンマーク出版)、『水の「真」力』『水は語る (文庫版)』(講談社)、『水が伝える愛のかたち』(徳間書店)、『水は音楽を聴いている』(三笠書房)、『波動時代への序幕』(サンロード出版) ほか 10 冊の波動関連書。

Author　Masaru Emoto

　Born in Yokohama in 1943. Graduated from the Department of Humanities and Sciences, Yokohama Municipal University, majoring in International Relations. Established I.H.M. Corporation in 1986. Received certification from the Open International University as a Doctor of Alternative Medicine in October 1992,. Subsequently introduced to Magnetic Resonance Analysis Equipment and micro cluster water in the US. He undertook extensive research of water from an original perspective and the result of his research, *The Message from Water* (HADO Kyoikusha) has been translated into seventeen languages and created a great sensation. As a pioneer of HADO technology, he is also recognized as a leading propagator of HADO in Japan. He has been active in giving lectures both in Japan and overseas. He is currently the head of IHM Research Institute, the President of I.H.M. Co., Ltd., and the chief representative and chairman of the International HADO Fellowship.

　He is the author of *The Message from Water Vol.1*, *The Message from Water Vol.2*, *The Message from Life*, *What Water Tells Us* from HADO Kyoikusha, *Water Knows the Answer Vol.1*, *Water Knows the Answer Vol.2*, *Crystal Story* from Sun Mark Publishing Inc., *True Power of Water*, *What Water Tells Us* (pocket edition), from Kodansha Publishers Ltd., *The Shape of Love that Water Tells Us* from Tokuma Shoten Publishing Co., Ltd., *Water Listens to Music* from Mikasa Shobo Co., Ltd., *Prelude to the HADO Age* from Sun Road Publishing, and ten other works pertaining to HADO.

訳者　八井 晶世　はちい まさよ

　金沢に生まれ、アメリカ合衆国に渡り、アイオワ州セントラル大学言語学部を卒業。大学にて英語、比較文化論講師のかたわら、通訳・翻訳活動を開始。1997 年より海外を取引先とする株式会社安全研にて勤務。筆者作『水は答えを知っている』をきっかけに水の結晶に魅せられ本書の翻訳を担当することになる。現在、石川県に在住、二児の母。

Translator　Masayo Hachii

　Born in Kanazawa and graduated from Central University of Iowa, USA, majoring in linguistics. While teaching English and cross-cultural courses in the universities, started translation and interpretation activities. Have been working at Anzenken Corp., an international business oriented organization since 1997. Having encountered the author's book, *The Water Knows the Answer* (Sun Mark Publishing Inc.), the attraction of water crystals led her to take the opportunity to translate this book. Currently lives in Ishikawa, Japan. She is the mother of two children.

参考にさせていただきました／Many thanks for these references

CD
「黒人音楽の伝統　ゴスペル（The Glorious History Of Black Music）」AMUSE MEDIA ／ "The Glorious History of Black Music" AMUSE MEDIA
「LENNON LEGEND」東芝ＥＭＩ／ "LENNON LEGEND" TOSHIBA-EMI Ltd.
「天台声明　金剛曼荼羅供」DENON ／ "Tendai Shomyo, Kongokai Mandala Kyo" DENON Ltd.
スーザン・オズボーン「浜辺の歌〜ベストセレクション」Canyon International ／
"At the Shore(Hamabeno-uta) 〜 Best Collection" by Suzan Osbourne Canyon International
「君が代のすべて」KING RECORDS ／ "All about Kimigayo" KING RECORDS
「クリスマスベスト／ストリングオーケストラ」CX130 STEREO ／ "Christmas Best/String Orchestra" CX130 STEREO

本／BOOK
「世界遺産」昭文社／ *World Heritage* Shobunsha Publications,Inc.
「日本美術全集　曼荼羅と来迎図」講談社／ *Complete Japanese Art Works, Mandala and Raigozu* Kodansha Publishers Ltd.
「世界遺跡地図」コリン・ウィルソン、三省堂／ *World Heritage Map* Colin Wilson, SANSEIDO publishing co.,ltd.

その他／Other things
「救霊符」井上修／ "Kyureifu" Osamu Inoue
「スカトー寺の風景写真」写真家：川口正志／ "Landscape Pictures of Sukato Temple" Photographer: Masashi Kawaguchi
「和」の文字　書家：若山象風／ The Character "Wa" Calligrapher: Shofu Wakayama
「言葉のちから」（果物の実験写真）都まどか／ "The Power of Words" (Pictures of Fruit Experiment) Madoka Miyako

自分を愛するということ
水からの伝言 Vol.3

発行日	2004 年 2 月 22 日第 1 版　第 1 刷発行
著者	江本勝
撮影	IHM 総合研究所 木津孝誠 池田聖子　大井田洋　押手孝行　勝亦健 二村潤　佐藤誠哉　田中みぎわ
発行者	江本和子
発行所	（株）波動教育社 〒 111-0052 東京都台東区柳橋 1-1-11 イーストサイド ビル 1F Tel.03-3866-3592
発売元	（株）I.H.M. 〒 111-0052 東京都台東区柳橋 1-1-11 イーストサイド ビル 1F Tel.03-3863-0211　Fax.03-3866-5353 http://www.hado.com ヨーロッパ事務所 Hado Publishing B.V. Sluisvaart 66 1191HE Ouderkerk a/d Amstel The Netherlands tel.31-20-472-1838　Fax.31-20-472-1839 book@hado.net http://www.hado.net
翻訳	八井晶世
編集	真宗理香子　宇佐美百合
デザイン	望月孝彦　IHM NetDesign
写真	©Tsutomu Takasaki ／ amana images ©kanehisa Murakami ／ amana images ©Cross wave ／ amana images ©Masato Tokiwa ／ amana images
JASRAC	出 0400488-401
製版・印刷	株式会社　シナノ

落丁・乱丁本はお取替えいたします。
記事、写真などの転載についてはご一報ください。

Love Thyself
The Message from Water vol.3

Date of issue: February 22, 2004

Author: Masaru Emoto

Photography: IHM Research Institute
Takashige Kizu
Seiko Ikeda　Hiroshi Oida　Takayuki Oshide
Takeshi Katsumata　Jun Futamura　Masaya Sato
Migiwa Tanaka

Publisher: Kazuko Emoto

Publishing company: HADO Kyoikusha
East side bldg. 1F, 1-1-11, Yanagibashi, Taito-ku, Tokyo,
111-0052　Tel: 81-3-3866-3592

Sales agency: I.H.M. Co., Ltd.
East side bldg. 1F, 1-1-11, Yanagibashi, Taito-ku, Tokyo,
111-0052　Tel: 81-3-3863-0211　Fax: 81-3-3866-5353
http://www.hado.com

European office: Hado Publishing B.V.
Sluisvaat 66
1191HE Ouderkerk a/d Amstel The Netherlands
Tel: 31-20-472-1838　Fax: 31-20-472-1839
book@hado.net
http://www.hado.net

Translation: Masayo Hachii

Compilation: Rikako Mamune　Yuri Usami

Book design: Takahiko Mochizuki, IHM NetDesign

Photograph: ©TSUTOMU TAKASAKI ／ amana images
©KANEHISA MURAKAMI ／ amana images
©CROSS WAVE ／ amana images
©KAZUO KAWAI ／ amana images

JASRAC: 0400488-401

Typesetting・Printing: Shinano Co., Ltd.